Human History

1000 Interesting Facts About Humans
from Ancient Times to the Present

Welcome Aboard, Check Out This Limited-Time Free Bonus!

Ahoy, reader! Welcome to the Ahoy Publications family, and thanks for snagging a copy of this book! Since you've chosen to join us on this journey, we'd like to offer you something special.

Check out the link below for a FREE e-book filled with delightful facts about American History.

But that's not all - you'll also have access to our exclusive email list with even more free e-books and insider knowledge. Well, what are ye waiting for? Click the link below to join and set sail toward exciting adventures in American History.

Access your bonus here: https://ahoypublications.com/

Or, Scan the QR code!

Table of Contents

Introduction

Since the dawn of time, **humankind has been creating and innovating**. This book will take you on a journey **from the first human inventions to our current technological breakthroughs.** Journey into the past and explore how civilizations have evolved over thousands of years in response to their environments and experiences.

We start by examining some of **humanity's earliest innovations,** such as the **domestication of animals and the building of cities and civilizations**. Every century in history has seen advancements and major events, whether it be **the rise of Christianity or the barbarian invasions.** These milestones are useful ways to mark humankind's path toward progress.

By exploring these key developments, we can understand how past civilizations have shaped our current societies. So, join us as we explore the history of humans!

Early Human Migrations
(c. 200,000 BCE)

Explore our species' ancient history as we uncover twenty intriguing facts about early human migrations during the Stone Age. Learn how humans moved from their original home **in Africa** and adapted to changing environments.

1. Early humans moved around a lot. **They migrated from one place to another in search of food and resources.**

2. **Most early human migrations happened during the Stone Age**, a period that lasted for about 3.4 million years and ended in about 4000 BCE.

3. **During this period, people traveled across Africa, Europe, and Asia on foot or by boat** to find new places to live.

4. **In some cases, these migration patterns created connections between different parts of the world for the first time.**

5. **People used stone tools, such as hand axes and spear points,** for hunting animals or crafting weapons during their travels.

6. **Cave paintings were perhaps the earliest form of human artistic expression,** with the oldest ones being more than sixty-four thousand years ago.

7. **Early Homo sapiens evolved about 300,000 years ago in northern Africa before migrating out of Africa sometime after that.**

8. Some of the earliest human migration patterns included **traveling from Africa to Arabia and then India.**

9. **As humans spread around the world during this period,** they adapted their tools and lifestyles based on what resources were available in each new location.

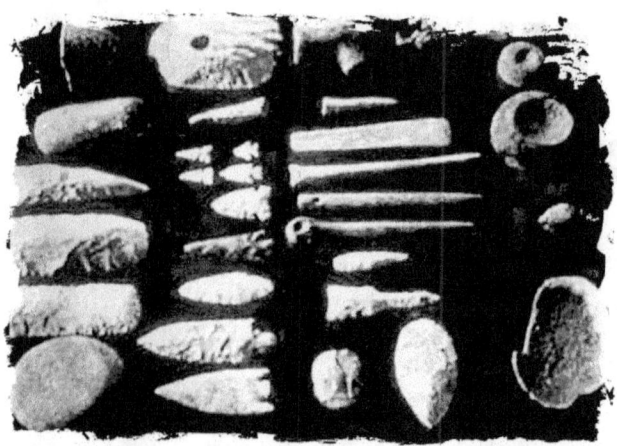

10. Archaeological findings suggest that **early migrations could have occurred across vast stretches of the ocean by boat** or rafts made from animal hides.

11. According to evidence, **climate change may have contributed to humans' long-term northward migration.**

12. It is thought that early humans took advantage of retreating ice sheets and crossed a land bridge between modern-day Russia and Alaska, **making it possible for them to migrate from Asia into North America.**

13. In addition to new experiences and adaptations, **early human migrations were important** since humans began the process of altering living environments in different regions across the world, resulting in distinct environmental or historical outcomes.

14. **The intermingling of cultures during this period helped people develop different languages,** customs, beliefs, and practices.

15. **Although some parts of the world were not explored** until much later (such as deserts or jungles that were hard to reach), **most continents had already been populated by humans** fifteen thousand years ago.

16. **Migration patterns created during the Stone Age** still influence many aspects of today's societies, including language distribution, genetics, and cultural customs.

17. **Genetic evidence suggests that humans from Asia and Europe** interbred during the Stone Age, leading to a mix of ancestries in many parts of the world.

18. **As different groups of humans came in contact with each other,** devastating outcomes occurred, such as war or the transmission of diseases.

19. **DNA analysis has shown that early humans** living in Australia were distinctively different from those in Africa and Eurasia.

20. **Early humans continued to migrate and evolve,** eventually leading to the modern human species that we are today.

First Human Inventions
(75,000– 1000 BCE)

This chapter **will explore the incredible inventions of our ancient ancestors between 75,000 and 1000 BCE.** These twenty fascinating facts will show you what was important to ancient people. **You might be shocked** at how many inventions you take for granted today!

21. **The earliest evidence of stone tools** has been dated to around three million years ago. Tools allowed people to hunt, cut, shape materials, and even make weapons.

22. **Fire was another vital invention that helped humans protect themselves from predators and cold weather.** They could also use fire to cook food, giving them better nutrition. People discovered fire hundreds of thousands of years ago.

23. **Controlling fire meant the invention of lamps,** which became common during this era. These lamps were not powered by electricity like our lamps today, but they did provide an efficient way to light dark areas.

24. **The Cave of Altamira has some of the oldest and most famous cave paintings in the world.** The cave is located in Spain, and the paintings date back to about 36,000 BCE.

25. **Up to 350 cave painting sites have been discovered in France and Spain** alone, signifying the importance of these paintings to early inhabitants of this region.

26. **Archaeologists have discovered thin, sharp bones** that are thought to be sewing needles dating as far back as 50,000 BCE in different parts of the world. **Needles allowed humans to create clothing from animal skins,** protecting them from harsh environmental conditions such as snow or rainstorms.

27. **Boats were invented during this period,** providing a more efficient way to travel across lakes, rivers, and oceans, leading to wider exploration by our ancestors into unknown lands.

28. **Ceramics were invented as early as 28,000 BCE,** allowing humans to create containers for their food and water.

29. **By 5000 BCE**, many important inventions had been made, including **musical instruments (such as flutes) and the wheel.** The exact dates of these inventions vary from region to region.

30. **People used ropes made of animal fibers** for construction projects or fishing nets.

31. **The bow and arrow is one of the most significant human inventions,** as it allowed our ancestors to hunt game from longer distances with greater accuracy than spears.

32. **Agriculture started around 10,000 BCE.** People planted seeds collected from wild plants into fields to grow crops to harvest, providing much-needed sustenance.

33. **Glass was first invented around 3500 BCE** and was originally used for artistic purposes.

34. **The pottery wheel is thought to have been first invented in Mesopotamia,** which was home to numerous firsts. Ancient Sumerians used the pottery wheel as early as 3250 BCE to shape clay vessels into various items, like pots, bowls, and jars.

35. **The invention of textiles allowed our ancestors to create clothing more efficiently by spinning fibers from animals** into yarn that could then be woven together using looms, giving them much warmer and more comfortable garments.

36. **Early metalworking began in about 6000 BCE,** which allowed humans to create stronger tools and weapons.

37. At first, metals like **copper and bronze were extensively used.** Later, **iron tools rose to prominence,** eventually replacing copper and bronze tools because of their durability.

38. Before paper was invented, people recorded information in different ways, including **carving stone tablets or writing on papyrus.**

39. **The earliest stone tablets were discovered in modern-day Iraq** and date back to c. 3500 BCE.

40. **A very basic mathematical system was used during this period.** Counting systems by making tally marks on bones, sticks, or stones have been discovered around the world.

The Domestication of Animals
(13,000–600 BCE)

Explore the fascinating history of animal domestication and its impact on human cultures. Discover how humans have adapted some species for their own needs and why the domestication of animals has been such a beneficial process with these twenty interesting facts.

41. **Domestication of animals is the process of taming wild animals for human use.**

42. **The first animal to be domesticated was the dog** around 13,000 BCE.

43. Other animals were domesticated soon after, **including goats, sheep, pigs, and cattle, in Asia and Europe** about eleven thousand years ago.

44. **Horses were among the earliest domesticated animals in Central Asia.** They were domesticated between 4500 and 3500 BCE.

45. Researchers believe **chickens were kept as pets or food sources in Southeast Asia around 3,500 years ago.** Some believe they were domesticated more like ten thousand years ago.

46. **Domestication allowed humans to have a more reliable source of food** since they could rely on certain herds or flocks instead of having to hunt prey every day.

47. **Domesticating animals meant that people could travel far distances without worrying** about where their next meal would come from because they had a steady supply with them at all times.

48. **The bond between humans and domesticated animals became so strong** that certain species were sometimes seen as family members or even gods in some cultures.

49. **People began using donkeys and horses to transport goods** overland while also utilizing them for plowing fields during planting seasons.

50. **Animals like cows, sheep, goats, and camels helped with agriculture** by providing milk or wool, among other things.

51. **Llamas and alpacas were used mainly in the Andes Mountains of South America** for their meat and fur and to help carry heavy loads up the mountainside.

52. **Cats were domesticated** ten thousand years ago in the Fertile Crescent.

53. **Dogs have been used by humans for many purposes,** including hunting, companionship, protection from predators, and helping to herd livestock like sheep and cattle.

54. **Bees are another example of an animal that has been successfully domesticated since around 9000 BCE.** They provide us with honey and help with the pollination of crops.

55. **Rabbits would not be actively kept as a food source until much later** during the Roman Republic. The first written records suggesting rabbit domestication in Europe date back to the 1st century BCE, though the animal was abundant in the region.

56. **Goats have been used by humans since at least 9000 BCE.** They were first tamed in the Middle East and provided milk and cheese, among other things.

57. **Pigs were one of the earliest animals to be domesticated.** People near modern-day Turkey domesticated pigs around nine thousand years ago. They are a valuable food source but can also be kept as pets.

58. **Sheep began being farmed for meat and wool** about eleven thousand years ago in the Fertile Crescent.

59. **Humans have used cows since approximately 8000 BCE** when they were first herded by our ancestors in India and Pakistan.

60. **Ducks were first domesticated in 2000 BCE in China** to provide eggs and feathers, but they can also be kept as pets.

The Creation of the First Cities
(7500–4000 BCE)

This chapter will **explore the fascinating history of the first cities.** We'll look at twenty interesting **facts about how these early settlements were developed,** and we will also talk about important ancient cities that impacted history.

61. By 7500 or 7000 BCE, **many people had started settling down together to form villages,** which eventually developed into large urban centers called cities.

62. **The first cities were built in the Middle East** and central Asia.

63. **These cities usually had a wall to protect them from invaders** and often had a temple or palace at their center.

64. **People living in these early cities developed new ways of producing food** that allowed them to support larger populations than before, such as herding animals for meat and milk products.

65. **Some of the earliest known cities are Çatalhöyük** (Turkey), **Jericho** (near Jerusalem), **Mohenjo-daro** (Pakistan), **Ur, Eridu, and Uruk** (these last three were in what is now Iraq).

66. Historians disagree on which city was the "first" city. **Most agree that Çatalhöyük was the oldest.**

67. These **first cities had public buildings, such as temples and palaces,** as well as markets and places where people could work.

68. **Ancient cities were usually divided into districts** according to the type of work taking place in each area, such as a residential district or an industrial zone.

69. **One of the most famous ancient cities was Babylon, located in modern-day Iraq.** Its legendary Hanging Gardens were considered one of the Seven Wonders of the Ancient World.

70. **In some cases, cities became so large that they needed to set up governments** with laws to keep order among their citizens; these developed civilizations.

71. **Early cities often built public projects like aqueducts or paved roads,** connecting them to other parts of their region or country.

72. **Some cities also traded goods with each other.** Spices from India were brought into **Mesopotamia**, while metal tools from **Anatolia** were found in **Africa**.

73. **Ancient city life was not always peaceful.** Wars between cities were common, especially over resources like land, water, or trade routes.

74. **Not all cities were built for war or settlement.** Some had religious purposes, like Göbekli Tepe.

75. **The rise of these early urban centers led to social changes,** with people living closer together than before and forming communities that could work together on projects more easily.

76. **This period saw a great deal of innovation from inventors who created tools and machines** that we still use today, such as pulleys, levers, plows, and wheeled carts.

77. **Cities often served as cultural hubs where different religious beliefs** could be shared and discussed and where art and music flourished.

78. **In some cases, cities even created systems of money** to help people trade goods more easily. Coins were first used in Asia Minor around 600 BCE.

79. **Ancient city life was not without its problems. Disease outbreaks,** food shortages, and environmental disasters could occur at any time.

80. Despite the challenges these early cities faced, **they are credited with laying the foundations for today's modern societies,** which have grown and expanded on those same principles of innovation.

The Rise of Ancient Civilizations

Explore the vibrant and complex cultures and civilizations of antiquity with this chapter as we delve into **twenty interesting facts about the powerful empires of Mesopotamia, Egypt, and China,** among others. This general overview of **the rise of civilizations** will give you a good foundation of how societies rose up. We will cover many of these civilizations in more depth later. Let us embark on an amazing journey through time and explore these **fascinating ancient civilizations!**

81. **Ancient civilizations started around 3500 BCE** in areas with fertile lands, like the Nile River Valley and Mesopotamia.

82. **The first ancient civilization was known as Sumer,** located in what is now southern Iraq.

83. **Other early civilizations included Egypt** (along the Nile), **India** (in the Indus Valley), and **China** (on the Yellow River).

84. **The ancient Egyptians were famous for creating monumental architecture, such as the pyramids,** which were used as tombs for their rulers.

85. **Ancient Rome was one of the most powerful civilizations of its time.** It emerged a bit later in the 8th century BCE and reached its peak in the 2nd century CE. Among its achievements was an extensive network of roads that **connected Europe to North Africa and Asia Minor** (modern-day Turkey).

86. **Ancient Greece was a prominent center of learning, culture, and philosophy** during its time.

87. **The Vedic period marks the end of the Indus Valley Civilization** in about 1500 BCE and the arrival of Indo-Aryan tribes in the region. They brought sacred ideas with them, the Vedas, hence the name for the period.

88. **In the Middle East, between 1300 and 612 BCE, Assyria rose to power,** becoming one of the most powerful empires of its time. This empire eventually fell after being conquered by **the Babylonians, who were later defeated by the Persians** (modern-day Iranians).

89. In Africa, **the ancient Nubian civilization rose to power around 2000 BCE** and is famous for its great monuments, such as the temples of Meroë, which still stand today.

90. **Ancient Chinese civilizations had a major impact on modern-day society through inventions like papermaking, gunpowder, the printing press, and the compass** (most of these were invented early on in the Common Era).

91. **The Maya civilization was one of the most advanced in Central America.** They developed an accurate calendar system.

92. **In South America, in the 12th century CE, the Inca Empire arose in Peru,** becoming one of the largest empires ever seen at its time (spanning over four thousand miles).

93. **The Aztecs, who rose to power in Mexico in the 1400s CE** and had a very advanced culture, developed hieroglyphic writing. Their intricate calendar system had a 260-day cycle; this calendar was known as tonalpohualli.

94. **Ancient civilizations developed unique systems of government, including monarchies** (like the Egyptians), **city-states** (like Athens), or **empires** (such as Assyria).

95. **Ancient societies believed gods controlled natural events** like storms, floods, and droughts. Many built temples dedicated to worshiping these deities.

96. **Trade between different ancient civilizations helped spread goods,** such as spices, fabrics, tools, and weapons, across vast distances of land.

97. **Ancient civilizations were often very creative,** producing artwork and literature that still inspires us today.

98. **The ancient Egyptians developed a complex writing system called hieroglyphs,** which were used to communicate on stone tablets or papyrus scrolls.

99. **The ancient Greeks laid the foundation for modern-day democracy.** In some city-states, citizens voted in assemblies on laws and policies that affected society.

100. **Archaeologists study ancient civilizations by digging up artifacts like pottery, tools, weapons, and coins.** These items help them learn more about how these societies lived centuries ago.

The Invention of the Wheel and Writing
(4500–3000 BCE)

This chapter will explore the incredible inventions of the wheel and writing in Mesopotamia between 3500 and 3000 BCE. We'll take a look at fifteen interesting facts about these monumental discoveries and how they led to improvements in other areas of society.

101. The wheel and writing were invented in Mesopotamia, an area primarily located between the Tigris and Euphrates rivers, between 4500 and 3000 BCE.

102. The main form of writing in Sumer was using a wedge-shaped tool called a stylus to create symbols on clay tablets.

103. The Sumerians developed cuneiform writing with wedge-shaped characters, which continued to be used until about 100 CE.

104. Writing systems evolved into syllabaries, where symbols represent the sounds of words, and then eventually into an alphabet that consists of letters that each symbolize a sound.

105. Writing made it possible for humans to share knowledge, ideas, and thoughts across different cultures or countries without having to talk face to face.

106. Ancient Mesopotamians also developed a system of measuring lengths that laid the foundations of modern mathematics today.

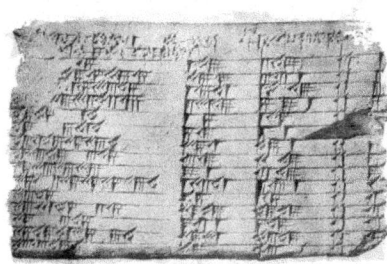

107. Cylinder seals have been identified from this period. They feature designs that are believed to represent either animals or gods, showing us how writing could be used for decoration.

108. It is believed the Sumerians were the first civilization to develop the wheel.

109. **Inventors figured out how to use round objects, such as logs, stones, and disks of wood with holes in them,** so they could attach spokes, making durable wooden wheels with axles.

110. **The invention of the wheel made it easier for people to transport goods** over long distances quickly and efficiently.

111. **Wheels were first used for pottery but later became part of chariots and other vehicles,** like carts or wagons, that could be pulled by animals or humans for transportation needs.

112. Before its invention, **transportation relied solely on animal power,** such as camels, donkeys, and horses.

113. **Writing made it possible for people to record their history,** laws, literature, science, and events in an organized way.

114. **Ancient Mesopotamia created roads paved with bricks,** enabling carts pulled by animals or humans to travel across long distances, making transportation faster.

115. **With the invention of writing,** people were able to trade goods more easily and create economic systems that allowed for **money or currency to be exchanged.**

The Bronze Age
(3300–1200 BCE)

Explore the captivating history of the Bronze Age and its wide-ranging impact on modern life. Get ready to delve into twenty interesting facts about how bronze changed how societies functioned.

116. **The Bronze Age was a time when people began to use bronze tools and weapons for the first time.**

117. **It was a time of great technological and cultural advancements** in various civilizations across Africa, Asia, and Europe.

118. **People used horses, donkeys, and oxen for transportation** and to pull carts or plow fields for farming during this era.

119. **Charcoal was burned in kilns to create bronze alloys** that would be shaped into tools or weapons, such as axes and swords, which were then sharpened using stones called whetstones.

120. **People in Bronze Age societies wore jewelry made from bronze,** gold, or silver, some of which have been found by archaeologists.

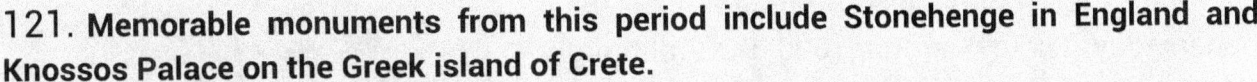

121. **Memorable monuments from this period include Stonehenge in England and Knossos Palace on the Greek island of Crete.**

122. Some of our modern religions trace their origin back to **Bronze Age religions. Judaism first emerged in Israel,** while **Hinduism began in India** during this period.

123. **The Bronze Age collapse, which occurred during the 12th century BCE,** remains one of the most compelling occurrences to date. Over the span of about one hundred years, almost all societies in **the eastern Mediterranean underwent a societal breakdown,** which affected their cultural and technological development.

124. **Mycenaean Greece, the Hittite Empire, the New Kingdom in Egypt,** and the Middle Assyrian Empire were all affected by the Bronze Age collapse.

125. **Iron tools were developed toward the end of the Bronze Age,** eventually leading to a new era called the Iron Age (1200–600 BCE).

126. **People in Bronze Age societies spoke many languages,** such as Sumerian in Mesopotamia, Mycenaean Greek in Greece, and Vedic Sanskrit (the language of Hinduism) in India.

127. **Many scientific inventions were made during the Bronze Age,** including sundials used to measure time.

128. **The Chinese invented writing during the Bronze Age, writing on something called oracle bones,** which were used to communicate with ancestors and the gods. Some scholars even believe Chinese was the first written language.

129. **Weavers used looms to create intricate textiles,** while goldsmiths crafted decorative items using precious metals like gold or silver.

130. **Astronomy became more advanced with the mapping of the stars by Babylonian astronomers,** who used their observations for divination purposes too.

131. **The invention of the potter's wheel in Mesopotamia** allowed for the mass production of pottery across the region.

132. **The first coins were minted in Lydia** (modern-day Turkey) around 600 BCE, although bartering was often used as an economic system during this period.

133. **In the Middle East, metalworkers crafted chariots during this period.** In England, people built hillforts to protect their communities from attack.

134. **Some of our modern sports, such as wrestling, javelin throwing, and boxing,** first emerged during this period.

135. **The oldest known legal code** was drawn up during the Bronze Age. It was called **the Code of Ur-Nammu.**

Ancient Mesopotamian Civilization
(c. 5000–539 BCE)

Explore the intriguing history of **ancient Mesopotamian civilization,** which existed in what is now **Iraq, Kuwait, Syria, and Turkey.** This chapter examines twenty interesting facts about the people who called this region home, including their beliefs, stories, and inventions.

136. **Mesopotamia is sometimes referred to as the Cradle of Civilization** because it was one of the first regions where people created complex societies.

137. **The main cities in ancient Mesopotamia were Uruk, Ur, Babylon, and Eridu.** These cities were all located near the Tigris and Euphrates Rivers.

138. **Many empires would call Mesopotamia home, including the Akkad, Babylonia, and Assyria,** which each had their distinct cultural characteristics, like languages and religious beliefs.

139. **People living in Mesopotamia developed farming,** allowing them to grow wheat and barley and domesticate animals.

140. **The Epic of Gilgamesh is an ancient poem from Mesopotamia** that tells a story about a heroic king who searches for immortality after his friend Enkidu dies.

141. **The Sumerian civilization developed a form of writing called cuneiform** that allowed them to communicate with each other. This innovation led to the development of ideograms later on.

142. **The ancient Mesopotamian religion was polytheistic,** with gods associated with different aspects, such as the **sky** (Anu), **fertility** (Inanna), or **water** (Enki).

143. **People from ancient Mesopotamia believed in an afterlife where their souls would go after death.** This mythical place was known as the Irkalla or the "Great Below" and was located under our world.

144. The Mesopotamians used math and astronomy for practical purposes, such as measuring time and predicting eclipses. They developed a base-60 system that was adopted by the Babylonians and is still used today.

145. Ancient Mesopotamia was divided into city-states that had kings or rulers who governed them with laws; some of these laws are still relevant today.

146. The Akkadian Empire is considered the first ancient empire. It was founded by a legendary ruler named **Sargon** and reached its peak in about 2200 BCE.

147. Art from ancient Mesopotamia includes statues, reliefs (stone carvings), pottery, cylinder seals, and jewelry that used precious stones like lapis lazuli or gold.

148. People in this civilization developed an irrigation system called a shaduf, which was a tool that could be used to move water from rivers onto fields for farming.

149. Music played a big role in society, with instruments like lyres being popular among the nobility. Drums were often used during festivals or ceremonies.

150. Economically speaking, trade was very important due to the availability of resources, such as minerals found near rivers. **Merchants traveled between cities to exchange goods** they had collected from different places.

151. Ancient Mesopotamians were skilled craftsmen who worked with a variety of materials to create tools, weapons, and jewelry. They used techniques like casting or inlaying stones into gold.

152. Doctors were able to diagnose illnesses by examining the body and prescribing treatments such as herbs or poultices.

153. Architecture played a huge role in Mesopotamian society, with impressive ziggurats (a type of pyramid) made out of mud bricks.

154. Several inventions originated in Mesopotamia, like the wheel, and are still used around the world today.

155. Babylon, a Mesopotamian civilization, was eventually conquered by the Persians in 539 BCE, ending Mesopotamia's time in the sun. The cultures from this region are still studied today as a reminder of how far human progress has come.

Ancient Egyptian Civilization
(3100– 30 BCE)

This chapter will explore **the rich history of the ancient Egyptian civilization.** We'll take a look at twenty interesting facts about their culture, beliefs, and arts.

156. **Ancient Egypt was one of the oldest civilizations in history,** rising to prominence in about 3100 BCE. The year of its conquest by the Romans in 30 BCE is considered its end date.

157. **Egyptians believed their pharaohs were gods** who ruled over them with divine power.

158. **As a sacred deity, the pharaoh was not only the ruler of the Egyptian people** but also the intermediary between them and the gods.

159. **The Egyptians believed in life after death,** so they preserved bodies through the process of mummification.

160. Just like our current calendar, **the Egyptians created a calendar with 12 months, each with 30 days, plus 5 extra days, making it 365 days long.**

161. **Ancient Egyptians were also great mathematicians** who studied geometry to measure land or build structures.

162. **The pharaoh's tomb was filled with treasure and artifacts** so they could use them in the afterlife, including furniture, food, jewelry, and clothes.

163. **The ancient Egyptians believed in many gods and goddesses,** such as **Ra** (the sun god), **Isis** (the goddess of motherhood), and **Anubis** (the god of death).

164. **The ancient Egyptians believed in magic and used it to heal diseases,** predict the future, or protect against evil forces.

165. **The Egyptian hieroglyphic writing system is one of the oldest known forms of written communication.**

166. The Egyptians were masters at building, as they created temples and tombs. **They also constructed boats,** which allowed them to explore faraway places like Africa and India.

167. The Nile River provided water for agriculture. People also used the river to transport goods and travel long distances.

168. The ancient Egyptians played various games, including senet (a board game), ball games similar to today's soccer and hockey, and javelin throwing.

169. Egyptian artisans were very skilled in making gold jewelry and creating intricately detailed designs using precious stones and gems.

170. The ancient Egyptians created pottery, sculptures, and paintings to celebrate their gods or commemorate life events.

171. The Great Pyramid at Giza is the only one of the Seven Wonders of the Ancient World to exist today. It was built around 2560 BCE.

172. Ancient Egyptian doctors used plants and herbs as medicines. Egyptians understood human anatomy because of the mummification process.

173. The Rosetta Stone, discovered in 1799, contains scripts in three languages, including a hieroglyphic message **written during the Ptolemaic** period that helped scholars decipher **the ancient Egyptian language.**

174. The Egyptians left behind countless artifacts, including papyrus scrolls with stories from mythology, **coffins carved with intricate designs,** and tall obelisks made out of granite, many of which still stand today.

175. The ancient Egyptians were among the first cultures to use coins as a form of currency, adopting it from the Lydians, who were the first civilization to mint coins in the 7th century BCE.

The Iron Age
(1200–550 BCE)

The Iron Age marked a pivotal point in human history. With the discovery of iron, people were able to craft larger structures and more powerful tools and weapons. **This period also saw the rise of many famous empires.** Let's discover twenty facts about this fascinating time.

176. **The Iron Age was a time in history between 1200 and 550 BCE** when people started using iron to create tools and weapons.

177. **The Iron Age in China began a bit later, around 600 BCE, during the reign of the Zhou dynasty.**

178. Before the Iron Age, **bronze was used to make tools and weapons because it was easier to shape than iron.**

179. **People eventually discovered that iron was much stronger than bronze.** Iron allowed people to create stronger weapons, like swords, axes, spears, and shields for protection against enemies.

180. **During this period, some of the world's most famous empires rose**, including the **Persian Empire** and **the Roman Empire,** both of which have shaped our modern world today.

181. **The transition to the Iron Age occurred after the Bronze Age collapse.** Some civilizations slowly rose back to stability after centuries of decline, thanks, in part, to the use of iron.

182. **New city-states began to emerge during the Iron Age**, some of which developed into powerful empires like those of Persia (modern-day Iran) and Assyria (modern-day Iraq).

183. **New agricultural tools had more developed designs, like iron sickles,** which have been found in multiple Iron Age sites in India.

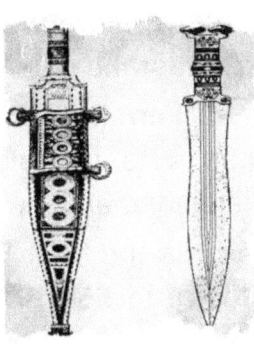

184. **Archaeologists have found evidence suggesting many Iron Age societies had complex political systems,** social hierarchies, and religious beliefs.

185. The Celtic people inhabited most of central and western Europe during this era. They were known for their fantastic artwork, metalwork, and jewelry.

186. Despite their prominence in the past, the Celtic languages are now only spoken in parts of northwestern France, Ireland, Wales, and Scotland.

187. The Iron Age saw great advances in technology, such as the development of coinage and other forms of currency and new means of travel, like ships.

188. Many hillforts were created during the Iron Age in England and other areas where Celtic peoples were located. The existence of these structures proves that the various Celtic tribes were heavily interconnected.

189. The Iron Age was also known for its beautiful pottery made from terracotta and decorated with geometric patterns or scenes depicting everyday life.

190. During this period, people began using written language more regularly than ever before. **Many scripts developed throughout Asia, Europe, and Africa.**

191. Bronzeworking techniques continued alongside ironworking throughout much of Europe until around 600 BCE, when iron became dominant due to its strength over bronze materials.

192. Iron Age art was highly symbolic and often represented gods, goddesses, or natural elements, such as the sun, moon, and stars.

193. The invention of iron tools made it possible to build massive structures like bridges that were strong enough to withstand river currents.

194. Farming during this era spread across Europe thanks to improved technology, leading to better crop yields and an increase in population.

195. In the Near East, t**he rise of the Persian Achaemenid Empire in 550 BCE is considered to be the "end" of the Iron Age,** while **Roman expansion in the 1st century CE is considered to be the end in Europe.**

Ancient Greek Civilization
(800—323 BCE)

This chapter will explore the fascinating history of the classical Greek period. We'll discover **twenty facts** about their **culture, arts, government, and religion.**

196. **The Aegean civilization refers collectively to several civilizations in ancient Greece during the Bronze Age** before its collapse around 1200 or 1000 BCE. It includes the Cycladic, Minoan, and Mycenaean civilizations. The classical Greek period began around 800 BCE and lasted until 323 BCE.

197. **The Greeks believed in many gods,** each with special powers and responsibilities.

198. **One of the most important gods was Zeus,** who ruled over all the other gods and goddesses from **Mount Olympus,** the highest mountain in Greece.

199. **Ancient Greek civilization was made up of several city-states like Athens, Corinth, and Sparta.** These city-states had their laws and governments; ancient Greece was not united except in times of war against foreign enemies. Many had similar cultures, but each city-state was unique.

200. **Ancient Greek architecture is famous for its beautiful temples dedicated to the gods,** such as **the Parthenon**, which was dedicated to **Athena**, or **the Temple of Poseidon** in Sounio.

201. **The first Olympic Games** happened in 776 BCE during a religious festival honoring the god Zeus.

202. **The ancient Greeks highly valued art and music.** They wrote plays about myths and legends, painted pottery and sculptures, and played musical instruments like the lyre and aulos (a wind instrument).

203. **Greek philosophers, such as Socrates, Plato, and Aristotle,** developed theories about knowledge, politics, science, mathematics, and ethics that have been influential in Western society for centuries.

204. **The ancient Greeks believed matter to have been made up of four elements: earth, air, fire, and water, also known as the classical elements.** A similar understanding of matter and life can be traced to other ancient civilizations around the world.

205. **The ancient Greeks were great sailors who explored the Mediterranean** Sea with their fleets of ships to trade goods with other cultures around them.

206. **The Greeks believed in balancing humors** (blood, phlegm, yellow bile, and black bile) through exercise and diet rather than surgery or medicine.

207. **Helen of Sparta's kidnapping by Paris of Troy legendarily sparked the Trojan War.** Historians still aren't sure if the Trojan War actually happened, although there is evidence that a city named Troy did exist.

208. **The ancient Greeks believed in many myths, like Pandora's box,** which warned people that curiosity could be dangerous if left unchecked.

209. The ancient Greeks made significant mathematical advancements, with **Euclid creating geometry and Pythagoras developing theories** about math and music.

210. **The ancient Greek language evolved throughout the centuries,** forming the modern Greek that is spoken today. Many English words are derived from Greek.

211. **Ancient Greece was the birthplace of the theater.** Tragedies and comedies were first performed on stage in Greece, often as a part of **religious festivals honoring Dionysus** (the god of wine).

212. **Sparta had one of the toughest military training systems.** Boys were trained from age seven to thirty to become strong warriors known as hoplites.

213. After the Bronze Age Collapse, the use of **writing in Greek territories was abandoned.** The Greek alphabet was developed around 800 BCE, ending centuries of life without a written language.

214. **The ancient Greeks believed in the power of "Arete," an ideal of excellence and achievement.**

215. **Greece would eventually be conquered by the Romans** in the 2nd century BCE and become a Roman province, though some parts would continue to be semi-autonomous. **The Roman conquest is considered the end of the ancient Greek civilization.**

Ancient Roman Civilization
(753 BCE–476 CE)

Explore **the rich history of ancient Rome**, and discover its powerful legacy that has left a lasting impression on our world today. In this chapter, we will uncover twenty fascinating **facts about Roman civilization**, including their **technology, government, and iconic structures.**

216. **Ancient Rome was a powerful and influential civilization** that lasted for over one thousand years.

217. **Romulus and Remus are the two mythical brothers who are said to have founded Rome** after being rescued by a she-wolf when they were babies.

218. **Roman technology was very advanced**. They built complex road systems, bridges, and aqueducts, some of which are still used today.

219. **Latin, the language of ancient Rome,** rose to prominence as **the Romans expanded from Italy and conquered Europe and the Near East.** Today, the Romance languages of French, Italian, Portuguese, Spanish, and Romanian all share Latin influences.

220. **Rome eventually ceased being a monarchy** in 509 BCE when its final king, **Tarquinius Superbus,** was overthrown. A representative **democracy** (a republic) was established.

221. **The Romans replaced the king with two consuls,** who would be elected to serve one-year terms. **The Senate was the most important legislative body** and was comprised of several hundred senators who served for life.

222. Consisting mainly of wealthy patricians, **the Senate's job was to vote on laws and make decisions for Rome.** The Senate's influence was diminished after Rome became an empire.

223. **Julius Caesar is perhaps the most famous ruler of Rome.** He brought about big changes to ancient Rome by essentially overthrowing the republic by becoming dictator for life.

224. **The Roman Republic would not officially end until 27 BCE when Caesar Augustus** (also known as Octavian), the adopted son and heir of Julius, became emperor.

225. The Colosseum in Rome is one of the most impressive structures from this period. People went there to watch gladiator fights and other shows.

226. People living in ancient Rome were divided into two classes: patricians (rich) and **plebeians** (poor). Initially, patricians held virtually all political power, while the plebeians' power was very limited. The plebians gained more power as time passed.

227. Religion played an important role during this time, with gods being honored in temples and through sacrifices and festivals.

228. Slaves were an important part of Roman society since they provided labor for many jobs that citizens wouldn't do or couldn't afford to pay for.

229. Education was highly valued during this period. A variety of schools taught subjects like literature, math, and science.

230. Gladiator fights were popular forms of entertainment in ancient Rome. Some men captured in war would become professional fighters. Later on, people could become famous by signing up to be a gladiator.

231. The Baths of Caracalla, with their huge open-air pools, were one of the most impressive structures in Rome.

232. Although the ancient Romans weren't the first to invent concrete, they were the first to use it on a large scale. **Romans mixed lime and volcanic ash with water, creating a material that is both strong and durable.**

233. The Circus Maximus was the largest chariot stadium in Rome. People would gather to watch chariot races and bet on the outcome.

234. Many famous monuments, such as **the Arch of Titus or the Arch of Constantine,** were built during this period to honor leaders.

235. One of the most influential aspects of ancient Rome was its legal system, which provided fair laws that applied to all provinces of the empire. This system was based on **the concept of natural law,** which held that law should be based on reason and justice rather than the arbitrary will of a ruler.

The Rise of Christianity
(1st Century—4th Century CE)

This chapter will explore the remarkable introduction of **Christianity beginning in the 1st century CE.** We'll examine twenty intriguing facts about this revolutionary period, including how **Jesus Christ's teachings spread** and some of the early influential figures in Christian history.

236. **Scholars believe Jesus Christ was born in Bethlehem, near the city of Jerusalem,** between 6 and 4 BCE.

237. **The early followers of Jesus were called Christians by others.** They spread Jesus's teachings throughout the Roman Empire.

238. **Many early Christians were baptized by John the Baptist.** Many scholars agree that **Jesus's** baptism in **the Jordan River by John the Baptist** is one of the most historically likely events of his life that the Bible mentions.

239. Before Christianity came to be, **most people across Europe followed different pagan and polytheistic religions** like those of the Greeks and Romans.

240. **After Jesus's death on the cross, some of his apostles wrote down stories about him,** which became part of what we know today as the New Testament. Some people believe the apostles did not write these stories, although that is the traditionally held belief.

241. **St. Peter, one of the Twelve Apostles of Jesus, was the founder of the church in Rome,** an institution that would later develop into the Roman Catholic Church and the papacy. For this reason, he is also considered to be the first pope.

242. **Paul was an important figure who helped spread Christian beliefs.** He traveled great distances and wrote letters that are now found in the New Testament.

243. **Many martyrs during this period gave their lives for their beliefs in Christ.** Their sacrifices are still remembered by Christians today around the world.

244. **After a vision from God, Roman Emperor Constantine I issued the Edict of Milan,** which made it possible for Christians to freely practice their religion in the empire.

245. **The Edict of Milan was not only concerned with Christianity;** it also granted freedom for any religion to be practiced, making it a very tolerant act.

246. **Emperor Constantine was one of the most influential emperors when it came to early Christianity's influence,** as he made Jesus the patron of his army and converted in 312.

247. **The earliest monasteries began springing up in the 4th century.** Monasteries are places where monks can come together to pray and study Christian scripture with one another.

248. **Saint Augustine** (354–430) was a significant figure who **contributed significantly to the development of the early church's knowledge of faith and theology** by writing a great deal about Christian teachings.

249. In 325 CE, **the First Council of Nicaea convened.** People debated many doctrinal issues in Christianity. Ultimately, it helped define Christianity as a unified religion with its own set of beliefs and practices that were accepted by the members present at the council.

250. **Early Christians began building places for gatherings and worship services, which allowed more people access to hearing God's word.**

251. **These buildings eventually had lavish decorations** depicting scenes from biblical stories meant to inspire those attending services there.

252. In 380 CE, **Emperor Theodosius declared Christianity Rome's official state religion,** giving it special privileges and support.

253. In 392, **Emperor Theodosius outlawed all non-Christian religious practices** and ordered that any temples or places of worship for those faiths be destroyed, leading to many holy sites being ruined.

254. **The five most important cities in early Christianity were** Jerusalem, Rome, Constantinople, Alexandria, and Antioch.

255. **Christianity has continued to spread and evolve over the centuries,** becoming one of the world's largest religions today, with millions of followers across the globe.

Barbarian Invasions
(5th Century–7th Century CE)

The barbarian invasions of Europe changed the face of the continent forever. These tribes disrupted Roman and other states' rules on a massive scale. Explore fifteen interesting facts **about the barbarian tribes,** including where they came from and who led them.

256. **Romans called groups of people from non-Roman cultures "barbarians."**

257. **The word "barbarian" comes from the Greek term for foreigners, meaning those who speak an unfamiliar language** or follow different customs. The Greeks even referred to the Romans as barbarians!

258. **Some barbarian interactions with the Roman Empire were peaceful,** while others resulted in huge battles and the destruction of cities.

259. **The Huns, Goths, Franks, Vandals, Lombards, and Alans were the prominent barbarian groups** that took part in the barbarian invasions during the final years of the Roman Empire.

260. **Many barbarian tribes came from central Asia and eastern Europe.**

261. **One famous barbarian invasion was led by Attila the Hun,** who threatened Rome between 441 and 451 CE.

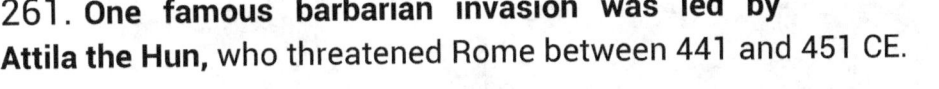

262. **The fall of the Western Roman Empire is often attributed to these barbarian invasions,** which weakened it over time.

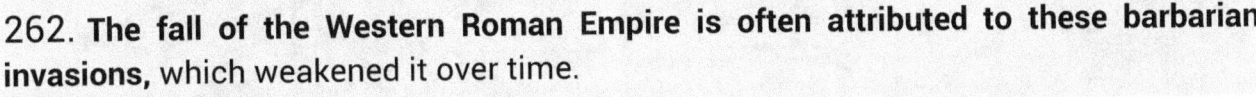

263. **The Saxons famously raided Britain around 450 CE** as a result of their exploits during various invasions.

264. **The barbarian invasions had a huge impact on the spread of Christianity in Europe,** as many tribes converted to the religion during this period.

265. **One of the most famous barbarian leaders was Clovis, King of the Franks,** who converted to Christianity in 496 CE.

266. **The Visigoths sacked Rome in 410 CE** and helped weaken it significantly.

267. One major result of these invasions was the formation of new kingdoms across Europe, such as **the Lombards creating the Kingdom of Italy.**

268. **Some barbarian groups, such as the Lombards, even adopted the Latin language** and writing system developed by the Romans.

269. **Linguistic studies have shown that many modern European languages are descended from those spoken by various barbarian tribes,** including the Germanic, Romance, and Slavic language families.

270. By the 7th century, **most of Europe had been divided among the different kingdoms formed by these invaders,** which lasted until the Late Middle Ages (1350–1500).

The Fall of the Western Roman Empire
(476 CE)

This chapter will explore the fall of the Western Roman Empire. We'll take a look at twenty interesting facts about its decline. **Why did the once-great Roman Empire fall?** And who or what was responsible for it?

271. **In the 2nd century CE, the Roman Empire reached its greatest extent,** occupying land not only in Italy and western Europe but also in the Balkans, Anatolia, Mesopotamia, Egypt, and Britain.

272. By the 4th century, **it had become clear that the Roman Empire was too large to govern.** In 395 CE, to deal with many of the governance problems, the empire was officially **divided into the East** (Byzantine) and **the West** (Rome).

273. **Rome was sacked by the Visigoths** in 410 CE, leading to its decline as a major power.

274. **The Huns invaded Italy** in 452 CE and caused further damage to imperial lands.

275. **Germanic tribes took over former Roman provinces** between 476 and 500 CE, with the Vandals taking over Carthage and the Ostrogoths occupying Sicily and Italy.

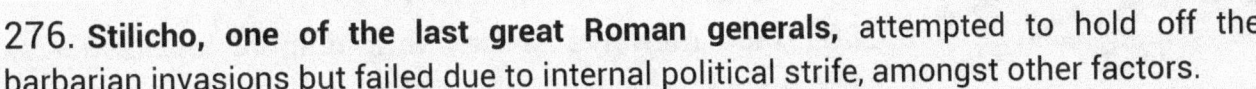

276. **Stilicho, one of the last great Roman generals,** attempted to hold off the barbarian invasions but failed due to internal political strife, amongst other factors.

277. **Romulus Augustulus is credited with being the last Western Roman emperor,** ruling slightly more than a year (475–476). He officially declared his abdication after he was overthrown by Odoacer, marking an end to the Western Roman Empire.

278. **The Eastern Roman Empire** (also known as the Byzantine Empire) lasted for around another one thousand years until its demise in 1453.

279. **Christianity, which became the official religion of Rome,** survived the collapse of the empire and continued to be very influential in post-Roman Europe.

280. By 476 CE, **a series of economic problems had arisen,** such as inflation and high taxation, leading to weakened infrastructure and military might.

281. **Political instability grew due to weak emperors being unable to keep strong control of territories under their rule.** Their ineffective rule allowed barbarian tribes to gain easier access to imperial lands without much resistance from government forces.

282. **Increased reliance on mercenary armies instead of full-time professional soldiers** made military efforts against enemy nations ineffective, which helped lead to Rome's ultimate downfall.

283. **The population decreased across different provinces due to plagues,** famines, and wars.

284. **The fall of the Western Roman Empire led to a long period of instability and turmoil in Europe,** with new kingdoms rising up and challenging each other for dominance in a world without a unifying empire.

285. **This period is often referred to as the Dark Ages,** although the name is now seen as a misnomer. However, there was a period of cultural and technological regression after Rome fell, and the region was stabilized by **the Renaissance.**

286. **Trade networks shifted toward more localized areas** since there was no empire to protect trade routes anymore.

287. **Germanic tribes began taking over lands formerly under the control of Rome,** introducing their language and laws in place of the Latin ones previously used by the Romans.

288. After 476 CE, **the former Roman provinces began to develop their own identities and cultures** that continue today in different parts of Europe.

289. **Feudalism became the dominant form of government in Europe** after the fall of Rome since it provided a sense of protection and stability.

290. **The church took over some power and authority from the state during this period,** leading to a rise in religious influence within society.

The Spread of Islam
(7th Century—Present)

This chapter will explore the incredible expansion of Islam throughout history and its many impacts on society, culture, art, and politics. We'll be looking at twenty facts about this fascinating religion that began on **the Arabian Peninsula** more than 1,400 years ago.

291. **Prophet Muhammad was born in 570 CE, and he received his first revelation from God in 610 CE.**

292. **Muslims believe there is only one God (Allah)** and that Muhammad is his messenger or prophet.

293. After receiving these revelations, **Muhammad started to preach about monotheism and social justice,** which were very different from the tribal traditions of Arabia at the time.

294. In 622 CE, due to increasing pressure on him from those who opposed his message, **he moved with his followers to Medina.**

295. **The year 622 marks the beginning of the Muslim calendar.**

296. In 661, **an empire called the Umayyad Caliphate was established.** It was the first Islamic dynasty. **The Umayyad Caliphate** expanded its territories, spreading Islam farther into central Asia and Europe.

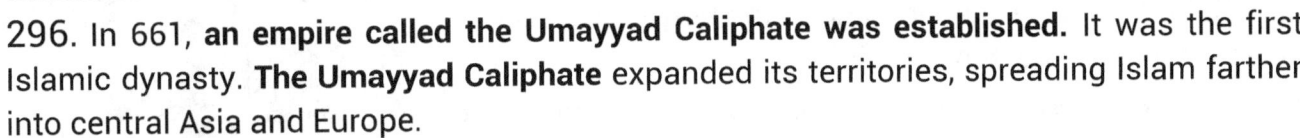

297. **During the first half of the 8th century, the Umayyad Caliphate conquered Iberia from the Visigothic Kingdom** and even tried to launch an invasion into France, only to be defeated by the Frankish forces led by Charles Martel at the Battle of Tours in 732.

298. **Islam spread quickly throughout most of southwest Asia following its establishment.** Muslims crossed into North Africa around 670 CE before reaching Spain by 711 CE.

299. **The Rashidun Caliphate captured the holy city of Jerusalem** after a long siege in 637. Jerusalem and the rest of **the Holy Land** would not be reclaimed by a dominant Christian power until the Crusades.

300. Beginning with **the reign of Caliph Harun al-Rashid in the 8th century and ending in the 13th century,** the Islamic world experienced a period of scientific, cultural, and economic excellence known as **the Islamic Golden Age.**

301. In 1258, **Baghdad was sacked by Mongol forces under Hulegu Khan,** leading to the decline of Islamic power in the region.

302. After that period, **there were several major waves of conversion to Islam,** such as during Ottoman rule (1299–1922).

303. **Today, almost two billion people practice this religion worldwide,** making it one of the largest religious groups.

304. **Islam blended with many diverse cultures across different parts of the world,** such as **the Arabic** culture **in North Africa and the Middle East, the Persian** culture in **Iran, and the Indian subcontinent culture.**

305. **Muslims are bound by an ethical code known as shariah,** which guides their conduct and is derived from the Quran and Sunnah teachings.

306. **They pay special attention to religious festivals like Eid al-Fitr, which marks the end of Ramadan,** or undertaking the Hajj, a pilgrimage to the holy city of Mecca at least once in a person's lifetime.

307. **Islamic art includes calligraphy, geometrical patterns, and arabesque designs** reflecting Islamic beliefs. Mosques, clothing, and manuscripts demonstrate the Muslims' keen eye for detail and beauty.

308. **Islam played an important role in changing Europe's political history when the Ottoman Empire expanded** in the 16th century CE. The flow of Asian goods into Europe was restricted and forced the Europeans to find a new route, which started the Age of Discovery.

309. **Countries with a considerable Muslim population today include Pakistan, Bangladesh, Indonesia, and India.** India is home to more than two hundred million Muslims, which is the most of any non-Muslim majority country.

310. **The spread of Islam has often been associated with violence and terrorism,** but this only accounts for a very small number of extremist groups that misinterpret the principles of Islam to suit their agendas or interests.

The Mongol Empire
(1206–1368)

Explore the remarkable history of one of **the largest empires in world history.** Let's explore twenty facts about **the Mongols,** from their ambitious founder to illustrious rulers like **Kublai Khan.**

311. **The Mongol Empire was the largest contiguous land empire in history,** stretching from the Sea of Japan to eastern Europe at its height.

312. **It was founded by Genghis Khan,** who united nomadic tribes under his rule and conquered many lands to form an empire.

313. **Another memorable Mongol ruler is Kublai Khan, the grandson of Genghis Khan.** He established the Yuan dynasty in China and ruled over most of eastern Asia.

314. During their conquests, **the Mongols developed new ways of communication,** such as the Yam system, which utilized messenger stations at certain intervals to quickly relay information.

315. **The Mongols had an efficient system for taxes,** which allowed them to fund their military campaigns without putting too much burden on people living within the borders of their empire, making it possible for them to expand even more.

316. **Their military tactics were very effective.** They often used feigned retreats or false surrenders to draw opponents into traps that would see large numbers killed with minimal losses on their side due to their excellent use of archers.

317. **The Mongols were infamous for their use of terror tactics,** often destroying whole cities to spread fear and ensure submission from potential opponents.

318. **The Mongols were experts at horseback riding** and were incredibly skilled at shooting arrows from atop their mount.

319. **Mongol general Subutai was one of the most distinguished Mongol warlords during the reign of Genghis Khan.** He led many campaigns and allegedly never lost a battle.

320. They built a vast network of trade routes that connected China with the Middle East and Europe, allowing goods like silk and spices to reach far-off lands!

321. Genghis Khan also established the first written legal code of the Mongols, the Yassa, which was used throughout his empire. It included laws about marriage, punishments, and property rights.

322. The Mongol Empire encouraged cultural exchange between different regions, bringing together people who shared knowledge on topics like medicine, philosophy, and religion, among others.

323. Under Kublai Khan's rule, Chinese culture flourished through literature and painting. He even built a grand palace in Beijing, the capital city of China.

324. The empire began to decline after Genghis Khan's death due to power struggles between his descendants and other leaders within it.

325. After the death of Genghis Khan, the conquered territories would be split by different Mongol warlords and generals. The southwestern part of the empire would be under the control of **the Ilkhanate,** which controlled the Near East and centered around **Persia. The northwestern** part of the empire spanned modern-day **Russia and parts of the central Asian steppe.** This region was overseen by **the Golden Horde.**

326. However, **many aspects of Mongolian culture remain today,** such as the language and customs practiced by certain tribes living near Mongolia's border regions.

327. In 1271, **Marco Polo, a Venetian merchant, visited China after traveling through Mongolia.** His account of his journey was written **by Rustichello da Pisa** in The Travels of Marco Polo. Despite the popularity of the book, there is no firm evidence that **Marco Polo** ever traveled to China.

328. The concept of Mongolian paper money originated during this period, as Kublai Khan issued currency to make trade easier throughout the empire over which he ruled.

329. The Mongols were known for their strict discipline. They often punished criminals severely while rewarding those who served loyally.

330. Even though it only lasted for about 160 years, the Mongol Empire changed world history with its advances in communication, trade networks, and military tactics that have been adopted by many nations since then.

The Middle Ages
(late 5th century—late 15th century)

A book on human history wouldn't be complete without a look at **the Middle Ages**. Many people write off **the Middle Ages** as a period of stagnation and backwardness. These twenty facts will show you just how interesting and formative this period really was.

331. **The Middle Ages, also known as the medieval period,** roughly lasted from the collapse of the Western Roman Empire to the late 15th century.

332. **There is not a single date when the Middle Ages ended,** but the fall of Constantinople in 1453 is often accepted as the end.

333. The Middle Ages is divided into three periods: **the Early, High, and Late Middle Ages.**

334. **The Early Middle Ages** lasted from around 5th to 10th century and is sometimes referred to as **the Dark Ages.**

335. **Europe became very unstable after the fall of Rome.** The population declined, trade fell, and the people lost the interconnectivity they had enjoyed in previous periods.

336. After **the fall of the Western Roman Empire in 476,** Rome's former territories were divided by the newly arriving **Germanic peoples**, who created their own states throughout Europe.

337. **The Christian Church would emerge as the most reputable authority in the Early Middle Ages.** The religion continued to spread and would be adopted by the new rulers in western Europe in the coming centuries.

338. **Christianity would develop somewhat differently in the West,** with the Church of Rome emerging as a rival to **the Church of Constantinople,** resulting in **the Great Schism** that saw the split of the church into **Roman** (Western) **Catholic** and **Greek** (Eastern) **Orthodox.**

339. **The Franks created a state in western Europe** that would eventually develop **into the Kingdom of France.**

340. **The most famous and accomplished Frankish ruler was Charlemagne,** or Charles the Great. He came to the Frankish throne in 768 and conquered territories in modern-day France, northern Italy, northeastern Spain, and western Germany, founding the Carolingian Empire.

341. In 800, **Charlemagne would be crowned emperor of the Romans by Pope Leo III in the city of Rome.**

342. **The High Middle Ages** began around the 10th century and lasted roughly until the year 1350.

343. **It was marked by an increasing rate of urbanization, the peak of feudalism,** the stabilization of state borders, and the beginning of rediscovering the classical past, which eventually ushered in the Renaissance.

344. **The High Middle Ages was also the era of the Crusades,** when European Christians launched multiple invasions against the Muslim-controlled lands in Palestine with the hopes of reclaiming Christian holy sites.

345. **The Reconquista took place parallel to the Crusades,** with the Christian factions hoping to defeat the Muslims in Iberia.

346. In the mid-14th century, **Europe was devastated by an outbreak of the bubonic plague,** commonly referred to as **the Black Death.**

347. Most likely spreading from the East, the Black Death wiped out about a third of the European population by the year 1350.

348. **The Late Middle Ages began after the Black Death** and ended with the fall of Constantinople in 1453.

349. **This period saw many major conflicts in Europe,** including **the famous Hundred Years' War between France and England and the rise of the Ottoman Empire,** which took over many of the territories formerly controlled by the Byzantine Empire.

350. **The most widespread form of political organization during the Middle Ages was the monarchy,** with only a few republics or oligarchies existing in Europe at the time, like Venice or Novgorod.

The Renaissance
(14th–17th Centuries CE)

This chapter will explore the incredible period of history known as the **Renaissance.** This was a time of **great progress in art, writing, music, science, and technology across Europe.** We'll discover twenty interesting facts about famous artists, writers, and inventors.

351. **The Renaissance was a period between the 14th and 17th** centuries when Europe experienced an explosion in art, writing, music, science, and technology.

352. **During the Renaissance, people began to explore new ideas about religion, politics, and human rights.**

353. Many famous artists lived during this time, including **Leonardo da Vinci,** whose works include **the Mona Lisa.**

354. **People were inspired by ancient Greek and Roman philosophy,** which focused on reason instead of faith or superstition.

355. **William Shakespeare** wrote many plays that are still popular today, such as Romeo and Juliet.

356. **Johannes Gutenberg developed a more efficient printing press,** which used movable type. The printing press allowed books to be printed faster and more cheaply than ever before.

357. **The printing press** allowed ideas from books, newspapers, magazines, and pamphlets to spread quickly across Europe and other places.

358. **Maps became much more accurate due to advances in cartography** (map-making) techniques.

359. **The writings of Niccolò Machiavelli helped shape modern political thought** by teaching power dynamics and strategies for rulers. His works, such as The Prince and the Discourses on Livy, provided a new way of looking at politics.

360. **People began to study anatomy and use microscopes,** which helped them gain a better understanding of the human body.

361. **One of the first operas was L'Orfeo, which was written by Claudio Monteverdi** in 1607. It is seen as the first major work of musical theater.

362. **Galileo Galilei used a telescope to observe planets for the very first time.** He discovered that Earth isn't the center of the universe but instead orbits the sun.

363. During this period, some new instruments, such as **violins, were invented,** allowing for a wider range of musical styles to be explored and developed.

364. **Renaissance art often features perspective drawings,** where objects become smaller as you move farther away from them.

365. **Relative stability and progress in Europe** led to the settlement of firmer borders, with various European kingdoms starting to advance their own national identities.

366. Some memorable rulers of this period **are King Louis XIV, who ruled France** from 1643 to 1715, **and Queen Elizabeth I, who ruled England** from 1558 to 1603.

367. **Banking developed into an important industry** due to economic innovations like double-entry bookkeeping.

368. **The Protestant Reformation began in the 16th century,** which led to a split between Catholics and Protestants.

369. **New architectural styles, such as Baroque, emerged during this time.** This architecture came with grand designs incorporating lavish ornamentation and ornate detailing.

370. Some historians see **the Thirty Years' War** (1618–1648) **as the end of the Renaissance era.** However, there is no actual end date for **the Renaissance**. Its teachings and ideas were advanced in the coming centuries by European thinkers and artists.

The Age of Exploration
(15th–17th Centuries CE)

The Age of Exploration, also known as the Age of Discovery, was a period of great adventure, danger, and discovery. **Famous explorers** ventured out in search of new lands and trade routes. Let's explore the impact of this pivotal period with these twenty interesting facts.

371. **During this time, explorers from many countries, primarily from Spain, Portugal, France, and Britain,** sailed around the world to find new lands and trade routes.

372. **Many European countries competed with each other to explore new lands,** which led to rivalries between nations for trading rights and resources.

373. **Christopher Columbus was one of the most famous explorers during this period.** He sailed across the Atlantic Ocean in 1492 to try to reach India but ended up discovering the Americas instead.

374. **Christopher Columbus made four voyages from Europe to America.** He discovered many islands like Cuba and Hispaniola on his journeys and explored Central and South America.

375. **Ferdinand Magellan was another famous explorer.** He led a voyage around the world for three years, starting in 1519. Many people still give him credit for being the first one to circumnavigate the globe even though he died before the journey ended.

376. By exploring foreign seas and distant lands, **Europeans found new sources of wealth like spices, gold, silver, and fur.** They even enslaved people from Africa and the Americas.

377. **Many diseases were spread during exploration.** The Europeans had built-up immunities to certain diseases, while natives had never experienced such diseases before. Millions of people died.

378. **Explorers made use of new technologies** like better **ships** with sails that allowed them to travel farther than before and advanced navigational tools, such as **compasses, for guidance.**

379. **Hernán Cortés was a Spanish conquistador who conquered most of Mexico** from 1519 to 1521. He is famous for bringing about the end of the Aztec civilization.

380. In 1588, **the Spanish Armada was sent to invade England but failed miserably** because of bad weather and the English navy's superior tactics. This marked an important **shift in power between Spain and England.** British colonization also began to take off after this point.

381. **Portuguese explorer Vasco da Gama led a voyage around Africa's Cape of Good Hope** in 1497, establishing direct contact with India.

382. **Vasco da Gama's voyage helped Portugal establish close trading ties with the Indian subcontinent.** These ties would last for centuries and result in a period of Portuguese economic dominance when it came to trading Eastern goods.

383. **Juan Ponce de León was a Spanish explorer who sailed to Florida looking for gold.** Instead, he found something even better: freshwater springs that were believed by some people to have healing properties.

384. **Jacques Cartier was a French explorer who organized three voyages to Canada**, which took place between 1534 and 1542. His explorations would eventually result in France establishing a foothold in Canada.

385. **The New World was named after Italian explorer Amerigo Vespucci,** who sailed along the east coast of South America in 1499.

386. **The Dutch navigator Willem Barentsz led three Arctic voyages** between 1594 and 1597, mapping much of northern Russia and Norway.

387. **Henry Hudson was an English explorer** who searched for an easier way to get from Europe to Asia. He discovered what is now known as Hudson Bay in 1610.

388. **English explorer Francis Drake became famous after circumnavigating the globe** between 1577 and 1580. He set sail in England and largely followed the route of Magellan.

389. **Bernardino de Sahagún wrote one of the earliest accounts about Native Americans.** He was sent to Mexico **by King Charles V** in 1529 and spent many years studying the **Aztecs,** which he eventually compiled into **the Florentine Codex.**

390. **The Age of Exploration was a time of great danger,** but it also opened up new opportunities for trade and cultural exchange between Europe and the rest of the world.

The Reformation
(1517)

The Reformation was a period of great religious and social transformations. This chapter will take an in-depth look at **the history, figures, reforms,** and effects of this era with these twenty fascinating facts.

391. **The Reformation was a religious, political, and social movement that began in Europe** during the 16th century.

392. **The Reformation challenged the authority of the Catholic Church** and questioned traditional beliefs about religion and morality.

393. **Martin Luther is credited as the one who started the Reformation.** He supposedly nailed his Ninety-five Theses to a church door in Germany in 1517.

394. **People wanted to reform** (or change) **some practices within Christianity,** such as selling indulgences or giving power to priests instead of God alone. Many saw these practices as unfair or wrong.

395. **Because of religious disagreements, books were burned,** homes were destroyed, ideas were persecuted, and lives were lost.

396. **The Protestant Reformation gave birth to new forms of worship like Lutheranism** and Calvinism throughout Germany, Scandinavia, Switzerland, and France.

397. In England, Henry VIII broke away from the Catholic Church and formed his own Anglican Church in 1534.

398. **The Counter-Reformation was a response to the Protestant Reformation,** as Catholics wanted to preserve their traditional beliefs and practices while also making changes where necessary.

399. **One of the Counter-Reformation's main figures was Ignatius Loyola.** He founded **the Society of Jesus** (Jesuits), which sought to reform Catholicism through education and missionary work.

400. Several religious documents helped guide Catholics and Protestants, like the Council of Trent, the Diet of Augsburg, and the Westminster Confession, among others.

401. The Dutch Republic became one of the most tolerant countries during this period, allowing people the freedom to practice any religion they wanted without persecution.

402. In Switzerland, John Calvin emerged as the leader of the Reformation in the city of Geneva. Calvinism became one of the most popular Protestant denominations.

403. Martin Luther translated the Bible into the German language so people could read it more easily. By doing this, Luther helped significantly increase literacy rates in Germany.

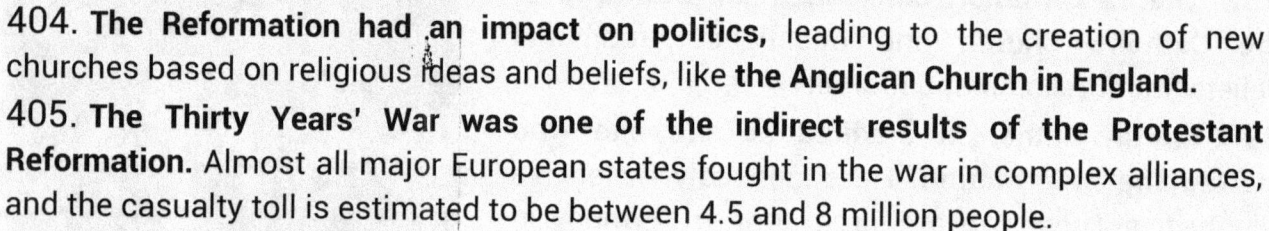

404. The Reformation had an impact on politics, leading to the creation of new churches based on religious ideas and beliefs, like **the Anglican Church in England.**

405. The Thirty Years' War was one of the indirect results of the Protestant Reformation. Almost all major European states fought in the war in complex alliances, and the casualty toll is estimated to be between 4.5 and 8 million people.

406. The Peace of Westphalia ended the Thirty Years' War, establishing the principle that the states of the Holy Roman Empire could decide what religion they wanted to practice without interference from others.

407. One of the most significant figures during this period was King James I, who authorized **the King James Bible for English-speaking** people in 1611.

408. Other leaders of **the Reformation include Swiss reformer Huldrych Zwingli,** whose teachings in the Swiss city of Zurich played an important part in the Swiss Reformation, as well as the development of Swiss nationalism.

409. By managing to make religion more accessible to people of all social strata, **the Reformation indirectly helped promote democratic ideals that European nations** adhere to today. This would be especially felt in the late 18th century.

410. All these changes had a great effect on the art and literature of the period, from the composition of **Protestant hymns** to paintings depicting Reformation themes like The Return of the Prodigal Son.

The Scientific Revolution
(16th–18th Centuries CE)

This chapter delves into the exciting history of **the Scientific Revolution**. We'll explore twenty incredible **facts about scientists and the discoveries** they made during this revolutionary time.

411. **The Scientific Revolution was a period when people began to use science and math** to learn more about the world around them.

412. **Astronomer Nicolaus Copernicus developed a theory that showed Earth wasn't the center of the universe.** Instead, Earth was one of many planets orbiting around the sun.

413. **Galileo Galilei helped prove Copernicus's theory** by using his telescope to observe our solar system from Earth.

414. **Astronomer Johannes Kepler discovered the laws of planetary motion** that explained how planets moved through space in an orderly way.

415. **Math genius René Descartes created Cartesian geometry**, a mathematical language for describing shapes on paper.

416. **The English scientist Robert Hooke used a microscope to discover the cell,** which is the basic unit of life.

417. **Dutch eyeglass maker Antonie van Leeuwenhoek built powerful microscopes** and became known as the **"Father of Microbiology"** after observing tiny organisms like bacteria and protozoa for the first time.

418. **Physicist Isaac Newton developed his theories on gravity and motion,** which explain how objects move through space.

419. **Scientist John Ray studied plants, animals, insects, and birds,** which led him to be one of the first scientists to recognize that all species have unique characteristics that make them different from other species.

420. **Francis Bacon wrote about new ways for people to think about nature using inductive reasoning,** a method where one draws conclusions based on observations rather than relying only on historical facts or traditional beliefs.

421. **British astronomer Edmond Halley was able to predict when a comet would return.** His prediction later came true, and the comet became known as Halley's Comet.

422. **Physicist Daniel Fahrenheit developed a new temperature scale** that is still used today to measure temperatures.

423. In 1735, **Swedish botanist Carl Linnaeus created a system for naming plants** and animals. This system is called taxonomy, and it's still being used today.

424. **British geologist James Hutton studied rocks and fossils to discover how Earth was formed.** His work led him to develop theories about how geological processes happen slowly over time rather than quickly during catastrophic events like floods or volcanoes.

425. **Chemist Joseph Priestly discovered oxygen,** an element essential for life that makes up about 21 percent of our atmosphere here on Earth.

426. **The French mathematician Pierre-Simon Laplace published his famous five-volume work,** Celestial Mechanics, which described how stars interact with each other using gravity.

427. **Physicist Alessandro Volta invented the electric battery,** which is still used to power all sorts of technology.

428. **British engineer James Watt developed new ways to use steam engines** and revolutionized the way people travel and do work.

429. **Chemist John Dalton discovered atoms,** tiny particles that form everything in our universe, from rocks to plants to animals, which helped lead him to develop a theory on an **atomic structure** that explains how elements interact with each other.

430. **English physician Edward Jenner created a vaccine for smallpox** that saved millions of lives by helping prevent outbreaks of the deadly disease.

The Age of Reason and the Enlightenment
(17th–18th Centuries CE)

Explore the period of **the Enlightenment** with us! This chapter will take a look at twenty interesting **facts that illustrate how this era marked a shift from superstition to rational thinking** about politics, society, and science.

431. **People during this time began expanding their horizons in science, technology, philosophy, and art.**

432. **They questioned traditional beliefs** and pushed for more freedom in society, including religious tolerance and individual rights like voting rights for citizens.

433. Famous people who helped lead this movement include **Isaac Newton** (scientist), **John Locke** (philosopher), **Montesquieu** (political philosopher), **Voltaire** (writer), **Beethoven** (composer), and **Mozart** (composer).

434. **The Enlightenment was also called the Age of Reason** because people tried to use reason rather than tradition or religion when making decisions about how to live life or govern countries.

435. During this period, **books were printed with movable type**, allowing Enlightenment ideas to spread rapidly.

436. **The Enlightenment supported the idea of a person's freedom to think and express oneself.**

437. **This period saw the growth of capitalism** (an economic system based on buying and selling goods) and colonialism (countries taking over other territories).

438. **Scottish philosopher and economist Adam Smith wrote his massively influential Wealth of Nations,** in which he treated economics as an academic discipline, eventually paving the way for the development of classical libertarian free-market theory. Due to this, Smith is often referred to as the "Father of Economics."

439. The intellectual developments in the fields of politics and philosophy would eventually lead to **the rise of movements that opposed the absolute rule of monarchies.**

440. While some Enlightenment thinkers believed in the gradual and eventual abolition of slavery, **like Jefferson and Adam Smith, the Enlightenment also gave birth to a new way of thinking of slavery** as the justified domination of inferior races.

441. **Women had more opportunities than before** but were still mainly restricted to domestic roles like taking care of the home and family.

442. **More people began traveling around Europe,** so ideas spread quickly between different countries.

443. Art flourished, with many famous painters creating works that reflect thoughts from this era, such as **Dutch painter Johannes Vermeer's masterpiece The Milkmaid** in 1658.

444. Music was not just for entertainment but also expressed political beliefs. **Ludwig van Beethoven wrote his Symphony No. 9** (a choral symphony) about brotherhood among nations.

445. **Philosophers used reason to argue against laws or traditions** they thought were wrong, such as those that supported slavery and religious persecution.

446. **The Enlightenment challenged many of the traditionally held dogmas,** which led to the decline of religion, particularly the Catholic Church.

447. **People during this time believed that knowledge should be shared** and not just kept secret by a few people in power.

448. **Philosophers disagreed on many issues,** but they all wanted to make life more enjoyable for everyone.

449. **The Enlightenment led to the start of the Industrial Revolution** (1760–1840), where new technologies changed how goods were made and distributed.

450. **This period was also very influential in starting the American Revolution** (1775–1783) when colonists declared their independence from British rule and formed a new country.

The American Revolution
(1775–1783)

From **the Declaration of Independence** to the adoption of **the United States Constitution,** this chapter explores twenty fascinating facts **about the American Revolution.** We'll discover important details such as who led the colonial army, famous battles fought during this time, and what role foreign countries played in securing freedom for Americans.

451. **The American Revolution** was a period of political and social upheaval in **the United States** that began in 1775.

452. **The war was fought between the British army and the colonists living in America** who wanted to gain independence from Britain.

453. **George Washington was the leader of the colonial army during the American Revolution** and later became America's first president.

454. **Thomas Jefferson was among the authors of an important document called the Declaration of Independence,** which declared that all people are equal and have certain rights like life, liberty, and the pursuit of happiness.

455. During this period, many famous battles took place, such as **Bunker Hill** (1775), **Trenton** (1776), **Saratoga** (1777), **Cowpens** (1781), and **Yorktown** (1781).

456. **The French, Spanish, and Dutch all helped the colonists** by providing supplies during the war.

457. **A spy network was formed during the revolution that provided important information to both sides.** Although **Paul Revere is best known for his famous ride** to warn the British were coming, he led a spy ring.

458. **Women played an important role in the American Revolution.** They worked on farms while their husbands were away fighting or took care of injured soldiers.

459. **It is estimated that about five thousand free black Americans fought for the revolutionary cause.** This number is relatively large considering that out of about 500,000 African Americans who lived in the Thirteen Colonies during the war, about 90 percent of them were enslaved.

460. In 1776, **the Second Continental Congress decided on the name the "United Colonies,"** which later transformed into the "United States of America."

461. **After winning several key battles against Britain, America finally gained its independence** with the signing of **the Treaty of Paris** in 1783.

462. It is estimated that **the American Revolutionary War** had a casualty toll of about sixty thousand. Although this number is small compared to other wars in Europe at the time, it is still relatively high considering the number of available military personnel in the Thirteen Colonies.

463. **The American flag is believed to have been first flown at Fort Schuyler,** but it was officially adopted on June 14th, 1777, now celebrated as Flag Day.

464. **Marquis de Lafayette was a French military officer who fought in the Continental Army under George Washington** during the war and helped the Americans achieve their independence. Later on, upon his return to France, he took part in the French Revolution, earning him a unique status as a hero of both revolutions.

465. **The American Revolution inspired other countries around the world to fight for their freedom as well,** like France, whose revolution started just a few years later.

466. After **America won its independence, it adopted the Constitution,** which determined how power should be divided between different branches of government. The US still uses its original Constitution today!

467. **The American Revolutionary War created new economic opportunities** for many people living in America at this time, such as merchants and farmers who started trading with Europe again after gaining independence from Britain's taxes.

468. With its resources depleted after years of fighting and in debt to nations like France and Spain, **the United States was put in a precarious situation. Conflict with the British** broke out again in 1812.

469. **The American Revolution brought about new ideas in government,** which eventually led to the creation of a democratic system, allowing citizens to have more rights and freedoms than ever before.

470. The outcome of **this war was extremely important for America's history,** leading it toward becoming one of the most powerful nations on Earth today.

The Industrial Revolution
(1760–1840)

The Industrial Revolution was a time of great change and technological advances that shaped the world as we know it today. This chapter will explore this period in depth, looking at twenty interesting facts about its innovations, effects on everyday life, and lasting legacies.

471. **The Industrial Revolution was a time when people started to use machines** to help make things more efficiently.

472. **The Industrial Revolution began in Britain** but soon spread around the world.

473. **New technologies, such as steam engines, railroads, and factories, were developed during this period,** which changed how goods were made and transported.

474. Before **the Industrial Revolution**, most products had been handmade by skilled artisans or craftspeople who used hand tools like hammers or chisels to shape materials into valuable items for sale at markets or shops.

475. **Improved farming methods allowed farmers to produce more food** than ever before, meaning people could move from rural areas into cities where they could work in factories making products.

476. **Inventions such as James Watt's steam engine helped power new industries** that created large amounts of wealth for factory owners while providing jobs for workers.

477. **Coal provided the energy needed** to power many of these new machines and factories.

478. **The invention of the spinning jenny enabled the production** of large quantities of thread and yarn in a shorter amount of time than ever before.

479. **The cotton gin made it possible for machines to separate cotton fibers** from their seeds quickly, increasing the demand for raw cotton, which was now cheaper to produce.

480. **Factory jobs were often dangerous.** Workers had long working hours with no holidays and minimal breaks provided by employers.

481. Some factory owners created living spaces called company towns, where **workers could live near the places they worked** while being subject to rules set by employers.

482. **Improved transportation networks allowed goods to be transported more cheaply and quickly over longer distances.** People could more easily buy products from around the world rather than just locally produced items.

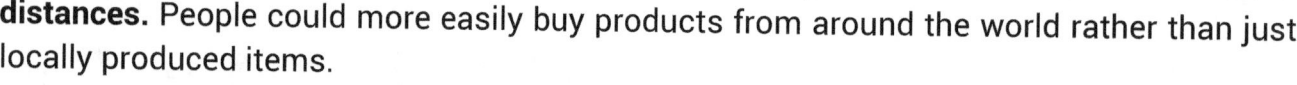

483. **The invention of the steamboat allowed goods to be transported quickly over large bodies of water,** such as oceans or rivers.

484. **Technological advances during this period** led to medical breakthroughs, including vaccines for several diseases.

485. **Industrialization caused a surge in population growth** due to improved living conditions and increased food availability.

486. **Working-class people eventually formed unions** to fight against unfair working practices and improve wages.

487. **Child labor was a common practice during this time,** with children often starting work at factories at a young age. **Most children began working** around eleven years old.

488. **The Industrial Revolution changed everyday life drastically.** It made products cheaper, but that came at a cost: polluted air and water, unhealthy working conditions, and poverty among workers who could not compete with machines for jobs.

489. **The Industrial Revolution** paved the way for many of today's modern conveniences, such as cars and electricity.

490. **The Industrial Revolution marked the start of a new era in world history,** with an increased reliance on machines and technology that continues to this day.

The French Revolution and the Napoleonic Wars (1789–1815)

This chapter will take us on an exciting journey through **the French Revolution and the Napoleonic Wars,** two of the most pivotal events **in European history**. We'll explore twenty amazing facts about this period, from iconic figures like **Napoleon Bonaparte** to revolutions that shaped the world as we know it today.

491. **Many people in France wanted more freedom and less power for the king of France, King Louis XVI.**

492. During this period, **books about politics and philosophy became popular** among the citizens of France, helping spread ideas on democracy and freedom.

493. **People stormed a prison called Bastille** on July 14th, which is now celebrated as a holiday called **Bastille Day in France** every year.

494. **After storming the Bastille, many new laws were made** that gave people equal rights before the law, no matter their social class or wealth level.

495. In June 1791, **the royal family tried to flee France**. **King Louis XVI and Queen Marie Antoinette** would be stopped at the small town of Varennes and would be arrested by the revolutionaries.

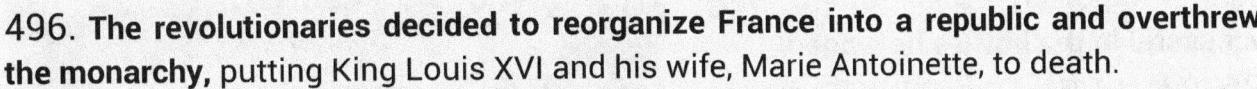

496. **The revolutionaries decided to reorganize France into a republic and overthrew the monarchy,** putting King Louis XVI and his wife, Marie Antoinette, to death.

497. According to legend, **Marie Antoinette once said, "Let them eat cake,"** when she heard her people were starving due to a lack of bread. However, it has been disputed if she ever said those words. They might have been attributed to her due to her unpopularity.

498. After the initial stage of **the French Revolution,** from September 1793 to July 1794, France experienced a period known as **the Reign of Terror**, during which tens of thousands of people who were suspected of being against the revolution were arrested by **the Committee of Public Safety.** Thousands of people were executed.

499. **The guillotine was widely used during the French Revolution** since it quickly decapitated people and was seen as less cruel than other punishments at the time, although it has since been banned from use due to its cruelty.

500. **The national anthem of France was written during the French Revolution** and is called "**La Marseillaise.**" It is still sung today.

501. **The French Revolution helped lead to other revolutions around the world,** such as the revolutions in Latin America.

502. **The first emperor of France was Napoleon Bonaparte,** who rose to power after overthrowing the French government.

503. **Napoleon changed many things about how Europe** looked politically, economically, and socially.

504. **Napoleon waged war against the European nations,** with his conquests taking him as far east as Russia.

505. **He wanted to make sure France reigned supreme,** so the country fought European countries like Britain, Spain, Austria, Russia, and Prussia to prove its might. **Napoleon was often very successful in the battles he waged.**

506. By 1815, **many European countries had allied to defeat Napoleon,**

bringing an end to the period of the French Revolution and the Napoleonic Wars.

507. **Napoleon was eventually defeated after losing the Battle of Waterloo in 1815.**

508. Even after **the defeat of Napoleon, France did not become a democratic republic**. Instead, the ruling Bourbon family was reinstituted by the winning allies.

509. **Many famous artists like Jacques-Louis David** were active during this period and painted portraits of important figures like **Napoleon Bonaparte.**

510. **The Napoleonic Wars changed Europe drastically by shifting borders,** establishing new countries, and creating different types of governments all over Europe.

The Wars of Spanish American Independence (1809–1825)

The wars of Spanish American independence were a tumultuous time in the history of Latin America. Spanning almost two decades, it saw people fight for their right to be free from Spanish rule and create **independent nations.** This chapter will explore twenty interesting **facts about this pivotal period,** including its key figures, the battles that took place, and the lasting legacy left by these wars on **Latin America's** economy and culture.

511. **The wars of Spanish American independence were fought between Spain and the colonies** it had in the Americas, such as **Mexico and Peru.**

512. **Many colonies wanted to be independent of Spain's rule** because of structural social oppression.

513. **An important leader of these wars was Simón Bolívar, a Venezuelan** military and political leader who led many battles against Spanish forces in South America.

514. **In Mexico, Miguel Hidalgo y Costilla began the fight for independence** by issuing the Grito de Dolores ("Cry of Dolores," the city where the call for arms took place) on September 16th, 1810.

515. **The people fighting for their freedom were called patriots or insurgents.** Some of the most patriots were José de San Martín, Bernardo O'Higgins, and Agustín Iturbide.

516. **A significant turning point in the Peruvian War** of Independence came when an army led by **General Antonio José de Sucre** defeated a much larger Spanish force at the **Battle of Ayacucho in 1824.** It brought an end to Spanish domination in South America and established **Gran Colombia and Peru as independent nations.**

517. **The country of Bolivia is named after Simón Bolívar.** He also helped liberate Colombia, Venezuela, Panama, Ecuador, and Peru.

518. **The Spanish wars for independence were greatly inspired by the American Revolution, the French Revolution, and the Haitian Revolution.**

519. **These wars for independence helped spread ideas** like freedom, self-determination, and nationalism across Latin America.

520. Some of the first independent nations created out of these wars were Venezuela and Paraguay in 1811.

521. Many battles were fought between independence fighters and loyalist forces who wanted to keep their colonies under Spanish control. Some famous battles include **La Paz** (1812), **Ayacucho** (1824), and **Carabobo** (1821).

522. The wars had a huge impact on the economy and culture of Latin America, with many cities destroyed and industries disrupted by the fighting.

523. These wars also provided an opportunity for Britain, France, and the United States to get involved and gain more influence over these new countries.

524. Spain would lose all of its colonies after the Spanish-American War in 1898, with the US gaining control of Puerto Rico and the Philippines.

525. The war saw advances in military tactics, such as guerrilla warfare, which involved small groups using surprise attacks against larger armies.

526. The heroes who fought during these wars are still celebrated today. Statues have been built across Latin America honoring them. Their stories have become an integral part of **Latin American culture**, and they remain a source of pride and inspiration for many citizens.

527. The legacy left by these battles is important too; they paved the way for democracy and modern government systems throughout **Latin America.**

528. The wars also inspired other countries to fight for their independence such as Greece and Serbia.

529. The customs, traditions, and cultures of the newly liberated nations of Latin America are similar to one another, owing to centuries of **Spanish colonial** domination that resulted in the assimilation of the peoples of these nations.

530. New countries were formed from territories that had previously been part of Spain's colonies. These countries include **Bolivia, Uruguay, Colombia, Ecuador, and Chile**, among others.

The Unification of Italy
(1859–1871)

Discover **the fascinating history of the unification of Italy.** In this chapter, you will explore fifteen facts about the unification process and the people who led the charge.

531. **The unification of Italy** happened between 1859 and 1871 when different regions combined to form one nation.

532. **The unification of Italy was led by a man named Giuseppe Garibaldi,** who became known as the "Hero of the Two Worlds."

533. By the time **Giuseppe Garibaldi became an Italian national hero**, he had already gained a lot of experience taking part in revolutions in Latin America, hence his nickname,

534. Before the unification of Italy, **the nation was divided into many smaller states** that were influenced by foreign powers like **Austria or France.**

535. After years of struggle and battles, on March 17th, 1861, most of **the Italian Peninsula was united** into one kingdom: **the Kingdom of Italy.**

536. **King Victor Emmanuel II became its first monarch,** with Turin as its capital city.

537. **During this period, there were two main political forces at work:** those for unification (led by Cavour, the prime minister of **the Kingdom of Sardinia-Piedmont**) and those against it (led by **Pope Pius IX**).

538. **One of the most important figures in the unification of Italy was Giuseppe Mazzini,** who founded Young Italy, an organization aimed at uniting people through education and culture.

539. The war for unification involved several battles, such as **the Battle of Solferino** in 1859, which helped secure Italian independence from Austrian rule; **the Battle of Volturno** in 1860, which ended the Bourbon reign over parts of Italy; and **the Battle of Mentana** in 1867, which crushed the last **resistance to unification.**

540. **In 1870, Rome was declared part of the unified Italian nation after French troops left it** following a plebiscite (a vote).

541. **The unification of Italy had an impact on culture** by bringing about new ideas from different regions, creating a unique national identity.

542. **The Italian language became more widely spoken during this period,** with many words borrowed from neighboring countries like France or Germany.

543. **Several laws were created to merge all of these minor states into one larger nation,** allowing for trade between areas and fostering the freedom of expression.

544. **Italy became a constitutional monarchy with a parliament** and limited suffrage, the latter of which was still pretty advanced for its time. **The monarchy** would later be abolished by the Fascists in the 20th century.

545. **The unification of Italy was a great achievement,** and it marked the start of modern-day Italy as we know it today.

The American Civil War
(1861–1865)

Learn about **the events that led to the outbreak of the American Civil War,** which changed the nation's political landscape forever. **These twenty facts will talk about the major battles and figures** involved during the conflict.

546. **The American Civil War was the deadliest in US history,** with over 600,000 soldiers killed during the conflict.

547. **The war was mainly fought between two sides: the Union** (also known as the North) **and the Confederacy** (or the South).

548. **Abraham Lincoln served as president of the United States** (the Union) for most of the war. **President Jefferson Davis** led the Confederate forces from Richmond, Virginia.

549. **The primary cause of this bloody conflict was slavery,** specifically whether or not it should be allowed to continue in America's new territories being formed at that time (such as Kansas).

550. **The first major battle took place near Manassas Junction, Virginia**, on July 21st, 1861. **The battle ended in a Confederate victory.** This conflict is often referred to as **the Battle of First Bull Run** by Northerners and **First Manassas by Southerners.**

551. Two of the most famous generals in US history, **Ulysses S. Grant and Robert E. Lee,** were both officers during the war and fought on opposing sides.

552. **The Union Army was larger than the Confederate Army** at a ratio of two to one, but it also had less morale and fewer supplies.

553. Several turning points occurred throughout the war that ultimately led to an overall **victory for Union forces.** These include **the Battle of Gettysburg** (July 1863) and **the Vicksburg campaign** (July 1863).

554. **The Confederacy used guerrilla tactics** to try to overcome its military disadvantages against its better-equipped opponents.

555. **The naval blockade imposed by the Union Navy** was a major factor in limiting supplies to Confederate forces and cutting off their ability to export goods for revenue.

556. **African Americans, both free and enslaved, played an important role in helping the Union forces** win the war. They provided intelligence and logistical support and even joined up as soldiers themselves.

557. **The Emancipation Proclamation, which was issued by President Lincoln** on January 1st, 1863, declared freedom for slaves living within all areas still under Confederate control.

558. **Women made valuable contributions during the Civil War.** Some served as nurses in army hospitals, while others disguised themselves so they could fight alongside men.

559. **The American Civil War** saw some of the earliest uses of industrialized warfare on land, including the mass production of weapons such as rifles and cannons.

560. In April 1865, **General Robert E. Lee surrendered his Army of Northern Virginia at Appomattox Court House in Virginia,** effectively ending all major hostilities on land between the two sides.

561. On December 6th, 1865, after years of bitter conflict, **slavery was officially abolished** with the ratification of **the Thirteenth Amendment** to the US Constitution.

562. **The Civil War is sometimes referred to as the Second American Revolution** due to its profound impact on society and politics within America.

563. Many famous Americans fought or served during the Civil War, including **President Rutherford B. Hayes, General William Tecumseh Sherman,** and author **Mark Twain.**

564. **This conflict saw the first use of air balloons for military reconnaissance purposes.**

565. After the war, a period known as **Reconstruction** began. Its purpose was **to reunite the North and South** economically and politically.

The Unification of Germany
(1866–1871)

This chapter will explore **the incredible history of German unification.** We'll take a look at twenty interesting facts about how Prussia unified the German-speaking states.

566. In 1871, Prussia led the unification of most German-speaking states, creating the German Empire.

567. The leader of Prussia at this time was Otto von Bismarck, who was also known as the Iron Chancellor because he had a strong will and ambition to unify **the German people.**

568. Before Germany's unification in 1871, it was made up of **several smaller states.** Though they were politically independent from each other, **they all considered themselves Germans** due to similarities in their cultures and societies.

569. Before the beginning of the military campaigns to unite Germany, Prussia led the smaller German states into a customs union known as the Zollverein, which integrated many German states into an economic zone.

570. One of the most important battles of German unification was **the Battle of Koniggratz,** which ended in a decisive **Prussian victory over Austria** in 1866 and led to the annexation of the **North German Confederation** by Prussia.

571. The new German nation adopted the Reichstag (parliament) as its legislative body. It still exists today!

572. In 1888, **Kaiser Wilhelm II became Kaiser** (emperor) of **the German Empire.** He ruled during WWI but was forced to abdicate when Germany lost the war.

573. As part of the unification process, **Germany established a new unified currency, the mark** (later replaced by the euro).

65

574. The unification of Germany made it one of the most powerful countries in Europe at the time and laid the foundations for future economic success.

575. The industrial development during this period was immense, with coal, steel, and other heavy industries being rapidly developed to support the increasing population's needs. **These advancements were essential for WWI,** which would happen around forty years after the German Empire was created.

576. In 1887, **Otto von Bismarck secured an agreement with Russia to isolate France.** This agreement became known as the Reinsurance Treaty.

577. German culture flourished during this era, with great achievements in art, literature, and music.

578. The unification of Germany brought about many changes to the education system. It was made compulsory for children between the ages of six and fourteen to attend school, and universities were opened to promote further education.

579. Germans embraced new technology during this period, such as railways, which allowed goods, people, and information to be transported quickly around the empire.

580. Berlin became the capital city of Germany and quickly became the most populous and largest city in Germany.

581. This period saw a rise in nationalist sentiment among Germans, with many believing that their culture and language should take priority over other European countries.

582. The Prussian Army was the core of Germany's military strength once it was united. The army managed to defeat both French and Austrian forces—two empires that were thought to be far more powerful than the newly created German state.

583. The unification of Germany also helped to foster the German language, with the language being spoken throughout the empire.

584. The unification of Germany caused an uproar in neighboring countries that had been at war with some German states in the past.

585. Germany's success in unifying its people and creating a powerful empire set an example for other European nations to follow, especially when it came to the military and economic merits of the Germans during this period.

World War I
(1914–1918)

Explore the tumultuous yet momentous **events of World War I, a devastating conflict that took millions of lives.** Discover twenty interesting facts about this **global war,** including what sparked it, its **major battles, new technologies**, and who was involved.

586. **World War I was fought between two sides: the Allies** (France, Russia, Italy, Great Britain, Japan, and, later, the United States) and **the Central Powers** (Germany, Austria-Hungary, and the Ottoman Empire).

587. **The Allies and Central Powers had several other nations on their side,** although they didn't provide as much support as the larger powers. **Some of the other nations that sided with the Allies include Serbia and Greece. Bulgaria aided the Central Powers.**

588. **The assassination of Archduke Franz Ferdinand of Austria-Hungary was the spark that ignited the war,** although tensions had been rising in Europe, especially in the Balkan nations, for quite some time.

589. **The most famous battles of WWI were Gallipoli, Verdun, Isonzo, Tannenberg, and the Somme,** all resulting in millions of casualties on both sides combined.

590. WWI was the first major conflict to use tanks, airplanes, chemical weapons, and machine guns.

591. **New technologies like submarines and zeppelins** (airships) were used for the first time during WWI by Germany.

592. **Women played an important role in WWI.** They worked in factories producing munitions and other essential items needed by soldiers at war.

593. **Once the men returned home from the war, most women were let go from their jobs.** However, they had proven that they could handle a job and care for their children, laying the foundation for women to become more active in the workforce.

594. **The Red Baron, whose real name was Manfred von Richthofen,** was one of the most famous fighter pilots from Germany who flew during the war. He was credited with shooting down eighty enemy aircraft during his career.

595. **Australian and New Zealand forces joined** to form the ANZAC, which fought at Gallipoli.

596. **The first tanks were introduced by Britain in 1916** and helped turn the tide in land battles against German forces.

597. All sides suffered huge losses. **Estimates vary, but between fifteen and twenty-two million military personnel and civilians died.** Many more were left wounded.

598. **New tactics, including trench warfare, led to long periods spent underground for protection,** which caused psychological damage when the soldiers returned home.

599. **Poison gas was used extensively during World War I,** with an estimated 100,000 people dying due to these weapons.

600. **The United States decided to join the war on the side of the Allies after the infamous Zimmermann Telegram incident.** German Foreign Secretary Arthur Zimmermann secretly sent a telegram to Mexico, inviting the country to attack the neutral United States, which gave economic support to Great Britain.

601. In 1917, after **unsuccessful military campaigns and a revolution at home, Russia negotiated an exit from the war with Germany.** This decision was made by the new Bolshevik government of Russia, which signed the Brest-Litovsk Treaty in March 1918, ceding control of many of Russia's western territories.

602. **US President Woodrow Wilson proposed the Fourteen Points,** a plan that included open diplomacy, freedom of the seas, and the removal of economic barriers among nations as part of his efforts for peace at the end of the war.

603. **The fighting ended on November 11th, 1918.** This is now known **as Armistice Day or Remembrance Day** and is commemorated annually worldwide.

604. **The Treaty of Versailles officially ended World War I** on June 28th, 1919, five years after it began. **The treaty blamed Germany for starting the war** and put severe restrictions on the nation. The treaty would play a large part in the start of WWII.

605. **The League of Nations was created following the end of WWI** to bring countries together and prevent future wars. It was composed of a council of representatives from each member state and a secretariat to carry out its work.

The Russian Revolution
(1917–1923)

The Russian Revolution was a complex series of events that changed the course of history. From **an autocratic monarchy to a communist state,** this revolution had a profound and lasting impact on politics, culture, and society; let's see how with these twenty fascinating facts.

606. **The Russian Revolution began on March 8th, 1917**, when hundreds of thousands of people marched through the streets to protest their government's oppressive policies.

607. **A series of revolutions in Russia changed the government from an autocracy to a communist state called the Soviet Union.**

608. A popular slogan during the revolution was **"Peace, Land, and Bread,"** which shows what was the most important to the working class.

609. **Tsar Nicholas II was forced to abdicate his throne** during this uprising, ending over three hundred years of Romanov rule over Russia.

610. **The communist Bolshevik Party,** after having overthrown the tsar, seized power in November, beginning a five-year-long civil war, which it eventually won.

611. **The Romanov royal family was imprisoned**

and eventually executed by the Bolsheviks in July 1918 at the Ipatiev House in the city of Yekaterinburg. The murder of the royal family, including **Tsar Nicholas II, his wife Alexandra, and their five children,** and four other people from the royal entourage was initially covered up.

612. **The Bolshevik Party gained control over most aspects of life within Russia** and soon established the Soviet Union with its **Marxist-Leninist** principles as guidance for governing society and economy.

613. The people of Russia saw drastic changes, such as land reforms removing aristocratic land ownership rights, civil marriage being legalized (separating church and state), **the introduction of universal education,** and the establishment of labor rights.

614. The civil war that followed the revolution was a brutal conflict between the Red Army (Bolshevik) faction and **the White Army** (monarchist/tsarist) forces. Millions of people fought in the war.

615. The Soviet Union would emerge as a superpower and would try to spread communism to other parts of the world as part of its main agenda.

616. As soon **as the Bolsheviks started winning the Russian Civil War,** they began attacking and annexing neighboring countries, where they established sister communist republics.

617. In the end, fifteen countries would make up the Soviet Union: Russia, Ukraine, Belarus, Georgia, Azerbaijan, Armenia, Latvia, Lithuania, Estonia, Kazakhstan, Tajikistan, Uzbekistan, Kyrgyzstan, Turkmenistan, and Moldova.

618. In 1921, Lenin introduced the New Economic Policy (NEP), which brought back limited private enterprise while still keeping control over some aspects of Russia's economy.

619. After Lenin's death, a man named Joseph Stalin took power. He killed his political opponents and created an autocratic regime based on fear and terror through a secret police force called the KGB.

620. Many new industries were built, such as **steel mills and coal mines,** making **the Soviet Union** one of the most powerful states during the 1920s and 1930s.

621. Leon Trotsky, one of the leading revolutionaries alongside Lenin, would be forced into exile after Lenin's death in 1924. In exile, he continued to preach the socialist cause but blamed Stalin for usurping power in the USSR. In 1940, **Trotsky was murdered by Soviet secret** police in Mexico City.

622. Although **the Russian Revolution** produced some positive outcomes, like increased economic growth in industrialization and improved public health services, **Russians suffered greatly during Stalin's reign,** with millions dying due to his purges or famines created by agricultural policies.

623. The Soviet Union eventually collapsed in 1991 due to economic troubles, the rise of nationalism, and increasing discontent with one-party rule.

624. Today, there are still remnants from this period, such as the Russian language being used widely across eastern Europe and central Asia due to its dominance during the Soviet era.

625. The legacy of the Russian Revolution can be seen in art, literature, and politics, with some of the latter even in practice today.

The Rise of Fascism

(1920s–1940s)

This chapter will explore the dark and tumultuous history of the rise of fascism in Europe. We'll take a look at twenty interesting facts about fascist governments, their leaders, and their views.

626. **Fascism is an ultra-nationalist, authoritarian political ideology** that advocates for the creation of a strong state with a centralized government.

627. **The term was coined by Benito Mussolini** in Italy in 1919, and the idea spread to other countries.

628. **The National Socialist German Workers' Party** (the Nazi Party) in Germany is a notable example of a fascist party. It rose to power during the late 1920s and 1930s.

629. **Fascists regard their own nationality or ethnicity as superior to other ones.** Fascist ideology would often use minorities as scapegoats. The Jewish people are a prominent example of a group that was used as a scapegoat by a fascist regime.

630. **Fascists tend to be hostile toward communism,** seeing it as a threat to their way of life.

631. **Propaganda is extensively used by fascist governments to promote their values and discourage opposition.**

632. **Hitler's speeches were incredibly influential on people living under his regime at that time,** even though they now seem outdated or ridiculous looking back at them today.

633. In a way, fascism during the 1920s and 1930s was largely a **reaction to Europe's politics following World War I.**

634. **Fascist governments typically have one leader who holds ultimate power, like Mussolini in Italy or Hitler in Germany.**

635. Mussolini and Hitler focused on creating national pride, often through militaristic displays, such as military parades or speeches about patriotism.

636. Fascists believed that firm government control could help bring order back to society after the chaos of WWI, which led many countries into an economic depression.

637. The fascist powers were involved in multiple wars during this period. For instance, **Japan invaded China,** Italy attacked Ethiopia, and **Germany fought against most of Europe.**

638. **During World War II, Germany, Italy, and Japan allied together and fought together against the Allies.**

639. **Fascists used censorship to control the media** and often suppressed the opposition.

640. In Japan, the military was seen as superior to civilians, and the government viewed other nationalities as "lesser." Some argue whether Japan had a fascist government, with some saying that Japan did not have a distinct party dedicated to promoting fascist ideals.

641. **Hungary, Portugal, and Spain also adopted fascist governments** during the 20th century.

642. **The rise of fascism led to increased militarization and authoritarian rule across many European nations,** which caused significant damage both legally and morally.

643. **The rise of fascism led to World War II,** which killed more than seventy million people worldwide, making it one of the most devastating wars ever fought in history.

644. The main fascist leaders were eventually defeated in 1945 when the Allied forces won WWII and restored democracy to Europe.

645. **While the fascist regimes in Italy and Germany brought certain temporary economic and industrial gains,** any "positives" of fascism are easily overshadowed by the atrocities and war crimes these regimes committed.

The Great Depression
(1929–1939)

This chapter will explore the effects of one of **the greatest economic crises in modern history: the Great Depression.** We'll examine twenty interesting facts about this period, including how it started, its effects on families and the economy, and some creative ways people tried to make money during these difficult times.

646. **The Great Depression was a time of economic hardship in the world.** Almost every nation was affected by it.

647. **It was caused by the New York stock market crash** on October 29th, 1929 (also known as "Black Tuesday").

648. In 1933, at the peak of **the Great Depression, about a quarter of the American workforce was unemployed.** To date, that is the highest rate of US unemployment in its history.

649. **Between 1929 and 1933, the wages of those who didn't lose their jobs in the US fell significantly, about 42.5% on average.**

650. **Many people lost their jobs, homes, and savings during this period,** which made it hard for families to make ends meet.

651. **Millions of Americans became homeless** because they could not afford rent or mortgage payments.

652. **People turned toward inexpensive entertainment like movies, radio shows, and books** to take their minds off the tough times they faced daily.

653. **Bank runs were common throughout the Great Depression.** When customers feared their savings would be lost, they would line up outside banks, trying to withdraw all their money before it disappeared entirely.

654. **Many families in the US moved westward in search of new job opportunities** or better living conditions than what they could find back home.

655. **To cope with hunger during tough times, some Americans resorted to eating "Hoover stew,"** which was a combination of whatever food they had on hand.

656. **In the US, people banded together to form "Hoovervilles,"** makeshift towns made out of cardboard boxes and other materials that were named after **President Herbert Hoover.**

657. **The Dust Bowl also affected the Great Depression.** It was an environmental disaster caused by poor farming practices. Drought and high winds combined to create huge dust storms all over **the Great Plains.**

658. **During this time, children often worked odd jobs,** such as selling newspapers or shining shoes, to help their families financially.

659. **Many people lost their homes due to foreclosure,** which means banks took possession when borrowers couldn't keep up with payments anymore.

660. **To combat the effects of the Great Depression, US President Franklin D. Roosevelt initiated the New Deal,** which was a series of new government programs, such as Social Security and unemployment insurance, to help people get back on their feet financially.

661. In 1933, **following the implementation of these government initiatives, the US economy began to improve gradually,** but it would not start to properly recover until WWII broke out.

662. **By 1939, unemployment rates had dropped from 25 percent to 14 percent,** and the public sector had also taken on a larger role in the economy, with government spending increasing from $3.6 billion in 1933 to $9.4 billion in 1939.

663. **The economy slowly began recovering by 1940 because World War II** increased the demand for goods and services in the US.

664. **There were only a handful of countries where the Great Depression did not lead to almost total financial collapse, like Great Britain and China.** Interestingly, China avoided the market crash since it used the silver standard; **Britain and the Nordic** countries, where **the Great Depression also had little effect,** left the gold standard early on after the crash.

665. **Post-WWI Germany was hit the hardest out of any country in Europe.** Due to Germany's massive foreign debt and war reparations it had to pay after its loss in **the Great War,** the German economy was very fragile and was devastated by **the Great Depression**.

World War II
(1939–1945)

This chapter will explore the dark and violent history of World War II. We'll take a look at twenty **interesting facts about this war, including its causes, major battles, and important figures** involved in the conflict.

666. **World War II was the deadliest war in history, with over seventy million people killed.**

667. **Adolf Hitler rose to power in Germany** in 1933 when he was appointed chancellor. He quickly began to introduce radical changes.

668. **In 1939, Hitler started WWII when he invaded Poland.**

669. **The Allies,** which included countries like **the United States, Great Britain, France, and the Soviet Union,** fought against **Germany and Japan during WWII.**

670. **Over sixteen million Americans served in World War Two.** That is a large number, considering the US had a population of about 113 million at that time.

671. **The Battle of Britain was fought over British skies** from July to October 1940 between **the RAF** (British Royal Air Force) and **the Luftwaffe** (the German air force). This battle was a pivotal moment in WWII.

672. In 1941, **Japan attacked Pearl Harbor** and brought the United States into the war on the side of the Allies.

673. **The Battle of Stalingrad** (1942–1943) **was one of the most brutal battles ever fought.** Over one million people from both sides combined died.

674. **The Battle of Midway** (June 1942) was a decisive victory for **the United States against Japan in the Pacific.** This battle saw the US Navy sink four Japanese aircraft carriers while only one American carrier was lost in combat.

675. **The Allied forces captured Rome** on June 4th, 1944, after fierce fighting with German troops.

676. **D-Day, an event that marked a major turning point in World War II,** was an important day for the Allies as they invaded German-occupied France with over 150,000 soldiers on June 6th, 1944.

677. **World War Two in Europe ended when Allied forces captured Berlin** in the spring of 1945, forcing Germany to surrender unconditionally.

678. **Atomic bombs were dropped on Hiroshima and Nagasaki** in 1945 to end the war, with Japan surrendering shortly afterward.

679. **During WWII, many important inventions were created, such as radar, jet engines, penicillin, and more.**

680. **Anne Frank is famous for writing her diary while hiding from Nazis during WWII in Amsterdam.** She died

in a concentration camp, but the book was published posthumously. It is one of the most widely read books ever written; some say it is the second-most popular book after the Bible.

681. **The Holocaust was a terrible tragedy during WWII.** Millions of Jews and other minority groups were killed by the Nazis.

682. **Elie Wiesel, Nobel Peace Prize winner and Holocaust survivor,** wrote his famous book Night about his experiences during WWII. He described the horrors of being separated from loved ones and facing inhumane treatment at the hands of Nazi soldiers.

683. **During WWII, about seventy million people served in the military worldwide;** this number includes both Allied and Axis forces.

684. **Women played a big role during this war, working hard at home and abroad.** They worked in factories or as nurses. Women also fought in the war or did other things to support the war effort, such as code-breaking and acting as spies.

685. **The Nuremberg trials happened after the end of World War II.** Nazi war criminals were tried for their crimes against humanity.

The Cold War
(1945–1991)

This chapter will explore the turbulent history of the Cold War, a period of tension between the United States and the Soviet Union. We'll uncover twenty interesting facts about this era, including the issue surrounding **nuclear weapons, proxy wars, and diplomatic efforts** to bring peace.

686. **The Cold War began when the United States and the Soviet Union could not agree on how Germany should be divided after World War II** ended in 1945.

687. **Another point of contention between these world powers was over ideologies.** The Soviet Union wanted to spread communism around the world, something that threatened the democratic principles propagated by the United States.

688. **Both sides had nuclear weapons, which made the Cold War very dangerous.** Luckily, no direct armed confrontation between the Soviets and Americans took place, and nuclear weapons were not used.

689. Still, **both sides participated in proxy wars against each other,** funding and taking part in various civil wars and revolutions to install regimes that would prevent the other from further spreading their ideology.

690. **Economic competition was also a significant part of this conflict.** The US followed capitalist principles, while the Soviet Union followed public ownership principles.

691. Some famous moments during this conflict include **President John F. Kennedy's speech at Rice University** (1962), **the Cuban Missile Crisis** (1962), **the Berlin Wall** going up in 1961 and coming down in 1989; **the Korean War** (1950–1953), and **the Vietnam War** (1959–1975).

692. In 1947, **George Marshall announced his plan to help rebuild Europe after World War II.** It was called **the Marshall Plan.** It helped Western countries recover economically. The US wanted to ensure that these countries could stand against the tide of communism.

693. **The Berlin Airlift** happened in 1948 when **the Soviets blocked off all access routes from West Berlin.** The West responded quickly with airlifts providing food and supplies until the blockade was lifted again months later.

694. In 1949, **NATO** (the North Atlantic Treaty Organization) **was formed by Western countries** to protect each other from any possible attack from the Soviets.

695. **The Communist Eastern European states were organized through the leadership of the Soviet Union** into a defense treaty called the Warsaw Pact to counterbalance against NATO.

696. **The Cold War was not only a military stand-off.** The two sides competed against each other in other fields, most notably sports and space.

697. **The Space Race saw the US and the Soviet Union compete to achieve dominance when it came to space.**

698. Many espionage activities from both sides occurred during this time. **Information was stolen or gathered illegally by governments** for their use, which added more tension.

699. **Radio Free Europe and Voice of America were two radio programs developed by the United States** that broadcast news about freedom and democracy to Eastern European countries to make people aware of what was happening outside their borders.

700. **Both countries built military bases in different parts of the world** to show off their power and strength. The US had Guantanamo Bay in Cuba, while the USSR had bases in Afghanistan.

701. **The Cold War created an arms race,** with both sides competing for more advanced weapons like nuclear missiles and submarines.

702. During the late 1960s and the 1970s, when the possibility of **the outbreak of war between the two sides was at its peak,** some American political figures wished to go back on the idealist vision of the war that fueled **the Cold War. The Nixon administration**, for example, wanted to increase public spending that was not directed to fighting the Cold War. This policy would be reversed by his successors, though.

703. **Many books, movies, and songs have been written about this era,** highlighting its effects on people's lives all over the world and showing how powerful political forces can be.

704. **Despite all the tensions, this period is remembered as one where science and technology advanced** rapidly due to the competition between both sides.

705. **The Cold War officially ended after the Soviet Union was dissolved.** Its communist government system collapsed, leading to the formation of new countries.

The Decolonization of Africa and Asia
(1950s–1970s)

This chapter will explore the process of decolonization and its impact on African and Asian countries. We'll look at twenty interesting facts about this period, including how colonial powers reacted to independence movements and strategies used by former colonies to gain freedom.

706. **Decolonization is the process of countries becoming independent from other countries' control, in this case, European control.**

707. **Colonies in Africa and Asia** were controlled by **France, Britain, Portugal, Belgium,** and other European nations before they gained their freedom.

708. In 1945, at the end of World War II, **most African and Asian countries were still under colonial rule** but began to fight for independence soon after the war's end.

709. After World War Two, **there was growing support for decolonization, as people wanted self-determination,** which would give them the right to choose how they would be governed without interference from outside powers.

710. **The United Nations supported this cause,** promising all people the right to govern themselves free from foreign domination or exploitation.

711. **Many African leaders used peaceful protests against colonialism,** while others took up arms to gain freedom from foreign rule. Nigeria's **Nnamdi Azikiwe** led a nonviolent campaign against British rule in the 1950s.

712. **India was one of the first countries to gain independence,** doing so on August 15th, 1947, after a struggle led by **Mahatma Gandhi and Jawaharlal Nehru** using nonviolent protests against British rule.

713. **Ghana became the first African country to gain independence from European colonizers** when it regained its freedom from Britain on March 6th, 1957. Kwame Nkrumah became its president.

714. Algeria won its freedom from France through an eight-year-long war that ended in 1962.

715. Vietnam is another example of successful decolonization, as the Vietnamese gained their independence following two wars: the First Indochina War against French colonial forces (1946–1954).

716. Decolonization had positive outcomes, such as the end of foreign rule and an increase in economic development, but there were negative outcomes as well, such as civil wars, ethnic conflicts, and political instability.

717. The process of decolonization took place over several decades, from the 1950s to the 1970s. Some places, like Namibia, would gain independence even later.

718. During this period, **many nations formed new governments** that were based on a democratic system that allowed for free elections and freedom of speech.

719. Decolonization led to increased pride among people living in former colonies who now had their own identities separate from European control.

720. In some cases, **European powers remained involved or interfered even after a country declared independence,** leading to further conflicts, such as the Congo Crisis (1960–1965).

721. South Africa managed to go through a long journey to complete independence from Britain, which the country achieved in the 1960s. However, even as a sovereign nation, it continued the harsh segregation practices against its black population, known as apartheid.

722. The leadership of political activist and statesman Nelson Mandela helped to end apartheid in the 1990s.

723. Decolonization also led to the formation of Malaysia, which was created in 1963 after separating from British rule.

724. During decolonization, some European powers refused to give up their colonies. Others recognized that it was time for them to let go and led negotiations for a peaceful transition of power.

725. The year 1960 is known as the Year of Africa, primarily because seventeen African nations gained their independence that year.

The Cuban Revolution
(1953—1959)

The Cuban Revolution was a momentous period in the history of Cuba. In this chapter, we will look at twenty facts about this historic revolution and its key players. Buckle up for a fascinating journey through one of modern history's most iconic revolutions!

726. **The Cuban Revolution** was **led by Fidel Castro.** He wanted to overthrow the government of **Fulgencio Batista in Cuba.**

727. **Fidel Castro, Che Guevara, and Camilo Cienfuegos were some of the key leaders** during the Cuban Revolution.

728. **The Cuban Revolutionary Armed Forces fought against the forces of President Batista's army** for several years until they finally won on January 1st, 1959, after defeating his last troops in Santa Clara, Cuba.

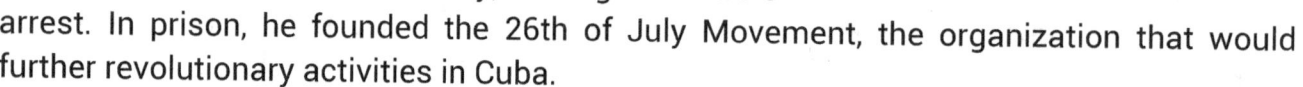

729. **Fidel Castro led an attack of about seventy rebels on the Moncada Barracks in Santiago** on July 26th, 1953, which failed miserably, leading to Castro's arrest. In prison, he founded the 26th of July Movement, the organization that would further revolutionary activities in Cuba.

730. **The 26th of July Movement would later transform into the Communist Party of Cuba.**

731. **Many people had grown unhappy with the dictatorship of Fulgencio Batista.** There was widespread corruption, and the president had links to organized crime.

732. From October 1957 to December 1958, **rebel leader Ernesto "Che" Guevara and his guerrilla army** of fewer than one hundred men and women marched across **the Sierra Maestra mountains in Cuba** to take critical cities from Batista's forces.

733. **Fidel Castro declared victory** on January 8th, 1959, after entering Havana.

734. **After gaining power, Castro quickly established a communist government** with himself as prime minister and **Che Guevara** as minister of industries.

735. **The Castro government nationalized most private property** in 1959, including foreign enterprises, such as oil companies and banks.

736. **The Cuban Revolution brought about numerous changes,** including land reforms that redistributed land owned by large landowners to poor peasants who worked for them.

737. **Universal healthcare was granted free of charge.** Education became free at all levels up until the university level, and many other social welfare programs were put in place, such as literacy campaigns in rural areas.

738. For the next few years after the end of the revolution in 1959, **hundreds of thousands of Cubans would flee the country due to the difficult sociopolitical situation there.** This event is referred to as the Cuban exodus.

739. **Most Cubans would settle in the US,** although Cubans migrated to other Latin American countries as well, such as **Puerto Rico** and **Mexico**.

740. **After the Cuban Revolution, Fidel Castro established close ties with the Soviet Union,** and Cuba's economy began to depend on it for trade.

741. **The US responded to the Cuban Revolution by cutting off all diplomatic ties with Cuba** and imposing an embargo on the Caribbean nation.

742. In 1961, **Fidel Castro declared Cuba to be a socialist state,** meaning that the government would control most aspects of citizens' lives, such as work and education.

743. During this period, **hundreds of thousands of political opponents were jailed or sent into exile,** while freedom of speech and freedom of assembly were restricted.

744. **Cuba also allied itself closely with other socialist countries like China and North Korea.**

745. **Revolutionary leader Che Guevara was executed** in 1967 during his attempt to spread a revolution in **Bolivia**.

The Space Race
(1955–1975)

Explore **the incredible history of space exploration with this chapter as we discover twenty interesting facts about the Space Race.** Learn how the US and the Soviet Union strived for supremacy and achieved some remarkable feats in the process!

746. **The Space Race was a competition between the United States and the Soviet Union to explore space.**

747. It began in the 1950s **when both countries wanted to prove their superiority** in science and technology.

748. In 1957, **the Soviet Union launched Sputnik 1,** becoming the first country to launch an artificial satellite into orbit around Earth. This launch showed that **the Soviets had mastered rocket technology.**

749. **Later that year, they sent a dog named Laika into space on board Sputnik 2**. She became the first animal ever to orbit Earth. The Soviets knew she would not make it back alive. Today, there are statues in Russia to commemorate her.

750. **President John F. Kennedy announced America's goal of putting a man on the moon before 1970.** This kickstarted NASA's **Apollo Program,** which was designed to develop the technology and resources needed for achieving this ambitious goal.

751. **The USSR and the US sent several unmanned lunar probes** to study the moon throughout the 1960s.

752. **The Soviet Union also put a woman named Valentina Tereshkova into space** in 1963. She became the first female astronaut to go to space.

753. In the 1960s, **both countries began work on a reusable spacecraft.** The US engineered **the Space Shuttle**, while the Soviet Union created **Buran,** which made its first unmanned flight to space and back in 1988.

754. In 1967, **Apollo 1 tragically caught fire during a practice launch, killing all three astronauts aboard.** The fire was caused by a combination of several factors, including a spark that ignited a build-up of pure oxygen in the cabin.

755. **America's first successful manned mission was Freedom 7,** which saw **Alan Shepard** become the first American to go to space.

756. **Apollo 11 launched from Cape Canaveral in July 1969.** Neil Armstrong, Edwin "Buzz" Aldrin, and Michael Collins were on board.

757. On July 20th, 1969, **Neil Armstrong became the first person ever to walk on the moon.** He said, "One small step for man; one giant leap for mankind," as he stepped off **Apollo 11** onto the moon's surface.

758. **The Soviets had beaten America in creating satellites, but the Americans are thought to have won the Space Race.**

759. In 1971, **America sent a probe called Mariner 9** to become the first craft ever to orbit another planet, Mars.

760. After 1975, **both countries stopped competing against each other and began cooperating on more peaceful projects.** This marked an end to the Space Race and a major shift in the Cold War.

761. **Both countries created spacecraft that could take people into orbit, such as Vostok 1** (Soviet Union) and **Freedom 7** (United States).

762. **Both countries have since cooperated on space missions, such as the International Space Station in 1998.**

763. **The Soviets and Americans sent unmanned probes to explore other planets in our solar system,** including Venus, Mars, and Saturn. This effort was part of a larger mission to explore the solar system and beyond.

764. **Both countries created powerful launch vehicles** that could take large spacecraft into deep space, such as **the Soyuz rocket** (USSR) and **Saturn V** (USA).

765. **The Soviet Union launched Proton-K rockets from Baikonur spaceport,** which is still used today for launching satellites. This spaceport is also used to launch **the International Space Station's** resupply vehicles and even human spaceflight missions.

The Vietnam War
(1955–1975)

The Vietnam War was one of the most significant events in modern history. This chapter will explore twenty interesting facts about this war, including its causes, effects on the people involved, key battles, and peace negotiations.

766. **The Vietnam War** was a long and costly war between North and South Vietnam that lasted from 1955 to 1975.

767. During the war, **the United States supported South Vietnam, while China and Russia helped North Vietnam.**

768. **It is estimated that around three million people were killed in the conflict,** including around fifty-eight thousand American soldiers and over two million Vietnamese soldiers and civilians on both sides of the conflict.

769. **President John F. Kennedy sent troops to help support South Vietnam** against communist forces from North Vietnam in 1961.

770. In 1964, **two US destroyers were attacked by North Vietnamese torpedo boats in what is known as the Gulf of Tonkin Incident,** prompting Congress to pass the Gulf of Tonkin Resolution, giving President Lyndon B. Johnson more power to begin bombing raids without declaring war.

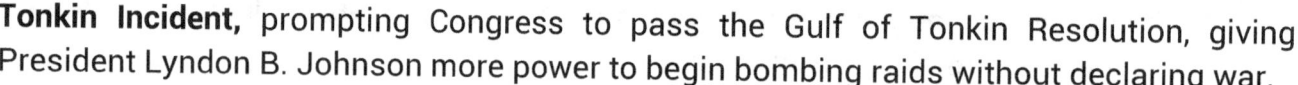

771. **Millions of refugees fled their homes due to political instability or violence during this period,** causing a humanitarian crisis.

772. **The Vietnam War, also known as the Second Indochina War** or the American War in Vietnam, was one of the most important proxy wars of the Cold War.

773. In 1968, during what became known as the Tet Offensive, **North Vietnamese forces captured several South Vietnamese cities,** causing an increase in US troops sent to support South Vietnam.

774. **Antiwar sentiment grew significantly among citizens from all countries involved,** especially in America, where large protests were held against the war.

775. **In 1968, peace negotiations began in Paris between the United States and North Vietnamese** representatives. The parties discussed the terms of the US withdrawing from Vietnam.

776. On January 27th, 1973, **both sides signed a peace accord that ended direct US involvement in the war.** However, this didn't end the violence entirely due to continued military activity.

777. **The last American soldier formally left South Vietnam in 1973,** although some private citizens remained for many years afterward.

778. In 1975, **North Vietnam conquered South Vietnam,** resulting in the reunification of the two states into one unified country.

779. In early 1979, **Vietnam was briefly drawn into a war with China.** Neither side emerged totally victorious from the war, and border clashes between the Chinese and Vietnamese troops would continue for many years.

780. **The Vietnam War was the longest and most expensive war for the US during the Cold War.**

781. **After North Vietnam's victory, the US severed diplomatic relations and imposed a trade embargo on Vietnam.** Relations would be restored during the Clinton administration in the 1990s.

782. **The use of defoliants, such as Agent Orange, by US forces caused severe environmental damage across Vietnam,** resulting in long-term health issues for the people living there.

783. **Medicines, food supplies, and other humanitarian aid sent by different countries** helped millions of refugees fleeing Southeast Asia during this period.

784. **The legacy of the war continues today through memorials, museums, and books** dedicated to those affected by it.

785. Since the war, **the United States provided financial assistance to war-torn Vietnam** and has continued to try and repair relations between the two countries.

The US Civil Rights Movement
(1955–1968)

This chapter will explore the important and often overlooked history of the US civil rights movement. We'll take a look at ten interesting facts about this period, including major events and the formation of crucial organizations that were led by influential leaders.

786. **The US civil rights movement** was a time of progress in the fight for equality and justice for African Americans.

787. **Black Americans were disenfranchised in the United States** despite having gained their freedom during the American Civil War.

788. **Many African Americans joined together to form organizations**, such as the Southern Christian Leadership Conference **(SCLC)** and the Student Nonviolent Coordinating Committee **(SNCC).**

789. **Dr. Martin Luther King Jr., Malcolm X, and other influential leaders** spoke out against racial injustice during this period.

790. **Thousands of marches and other forms of protest were held all over America** demanding equal rights for everyone regardless of race or color. One of the most famous marches was **the historic march from Selma to Montgomery, Alabama.**

791. In 1964, **Congress passed the Civil Rights Act,** which outlawed discrimination based on race, color, religion, or national origin in public places like schools, parks, and workplaces.

792. **The Voting Rights Act was passed in 1965.** This act sought to protect the voting rights of black Americans by outlawing discriminatory practices.

793. In 1968, **Congress passed the Fair Housing Act,** which stopped discrimination in housing and rental practices.

794. **School desegregation was also a major victory during this period,** as it led to greater integration in educational institutions for all students, regardless of race or color.

795. **The civil rights movement was a long and difficult struggle,** but it yielded very significant results for black Americans. However, instances of systemic racism and discrimination continue across **the United States** today and are some of the most challenging social problems America faces.

The Development of the Internet
(1960s—Present)

This chapter will explore the remarkable development of the internet since its invention in the 1960s. We'll look at seventeen fascinating facts detailing how it has grown and changed over time.

796. **The internet was invented in the late 1960s and has grown ever since.** It started as a military project called **ARPANET**, which was funded by the US government.

797. **The first web browser, NCSA Mosaic,** was developed and put into use in the 1990s. It greatly expanded on **the ARPANET** network and was engineered at the University of Illinois at Urbana-Champaign.

798. **By 1990, about three million people had access to the internet worldwide**. In 2000, the internet was used by more than four hundred million people worldwide.

799. In 1991, **Tim Berners-Lee created HTML** (hypertext markup language), which enabled people to easily transfer information between different types of computers all around the world, creating what we now know as the .

800. The year 1995 saw **Amazon** open its virtual doors. Initially, **Amazon sold books online. eBay followed suit shortly after;** both are still some of today's largest e-commerce sites.

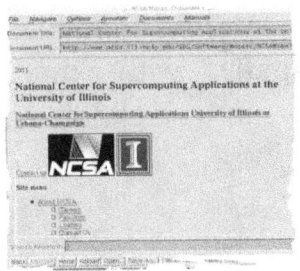

801. **In 1998, Google launched and quickly became the world's most popular search engine.**

802. **The development of smartphones further increased access to the internet** throughout the 2000s, with apps like Facebook launching in 2004 and Twitter (now called X) following suit two years later.

803. **YouTube launched in 2005,** giving anyone with a camera or smartphone an opportunity to share videos online for free.

804. **Smartphones have been replacing** computers as our main way of connecting online since their release in the 1990s. **Apple debuted its first iPhone in 2007,** revolutionizing how we use technology today.

805. **Social media grew rapidly during this period.** **Instagram** was founded in 2010, and **Snapchat** arrived on the scene in 2011.

806. **Streaming services such as Netflix also took off around this same time,** allowing users to watch movies and TV shows without having cable or satellite subscriptions.

807. **5G wireless networks began rolling out in 2018,** providing faster download and upload speeds than ever before.

808. In April 2023, **the global number of internet users surpassed five billion.**

809. **Artificial Intelligence (AI)** is now being used to improve our experience with the internet; this includes things like voice assistants and predictive search algorithms.

810. **The development of blockchain technology has created new ways for people to securely store and share data online** using decentralized networks instead of traditional central servers.

811. **Augmented and virtual reality** are also being used more and more to create immersive online experiences.

812. **Today, the internet continues to evolve rapidly** with more advancements in technology, making it faster and even easier for us to connect all over the world.

The Chinese Cultural Revolution
(1966–1976)

This chapter will take a close look at **the Cultural Revolution,** exploring its history and impacts on China. We'll learn **fifteen interesting facts that demonstrate** how this period of political and social upheaval changed life in China forever.

813. **The Cultural Revolution was a sociopolitical movement in China** from 1966 to 1976. It sought to "defend" communism by eliminating elements in Chinese culture and society that did not correspond to communist standards set by **Mao Zedong and the Communist Party.**

814. **The Cultural Revolution started when Mao Zedong,** the leader of China at the time, decided he wanted to reinforce his power and authority over the country.

815. During this time, **many people were persecuted for their beliefs** or backgrounds and had to flee their homes or be sent away to labor camps known as re-education centers.

816. **Traditional art, literature, and music were banned during this period** so they could not influence people's behavior.

817. **People destroyed ancient monuments** in an attempt to erase traditional values from society completely, even going as far as demolishing parts of **the Great Wall** of China itself.

818. **The "Mao suit" became a very popular piece of clothing** for males after the Communists' victory.

819. During this time, **students known as Red Guards were encouraged to report on and punish people who disagreed with Mao Zedong's ideas,** often leading to violent clashes between them and the police or other groups of citizens.

820. **The Cultural Revolution reinforced the personality cult of Mao Zedong,** as people were forced to see him as their savior and eternal leader.

821. **Many intellectuals were persecuted during this time** and sent off for re-education (or hard labor). Many were executed or died in the labor camps.

822. **A lot of private property and businesses were seized by the state during the Cultural Revolution.** This level of collectivization had devastating effects but was supposed to eliminate differences between different classes of Chinese society.

823. **People struggled for necessities due to a lack of supply caused by changes in society.** Some even resorted to eating tree bark just so they could survive another day.

824. **The Cultural Revolution lasted until 1976, when Mao Zedong passed away from illness.** His policies were reversed shortly afterward.

825. **The Chinese Cultural Revolution marked a major shift in China's history.** It transformed political structures, economic systems, traditional culture, and ways of life.

826. **It was a period of great suffering for many people,** leading to increased social inequality and political instability in the country, which still affects it today.

827. **The Cultural Revolution inspired similar policies in communist countries around the world,** such as those in Cuba and North Korea. However, its impacts were mostly felt within China due to its extreme nature and the length of time it lasted.

The Rapid Increase of Globalization
(1980s–Present)

The rise of globalization in the last few decades has completely changed how people interact with one another, share knowledge and resources, and do business across borders. **This chapter will explore fourteen interesting facts about this phenomenon.**

828. **Globalization is the idea that countries, cultures, and economies around the world are increasingly becoming connected** and intertwined.

829. Starting in the 1980s, **globalization began to increase rapidly due to advances in technology and transportation,** making it easier for goods, services, people, and ideas to be shared.

830. **The internet has made it possible for billions of people around the world to connect instantly.**

831. **This rapid growth in global connections has led to an increase in international trade** as well as investments between countries, creating a truly global economy where goods can flow freely across borders like never before.

832. **Globalization has also caused a large number of companies to move their operations abroad** in search of lower production costs or cheaper labor markets, resulting in millions of jobs being lost within developed countries while those same jobs are created elsewhere at much lower wages.

833. **International travel is now faster** and more convenient than ever before.

834. **Globalization has brought about a huge rise in cross-country migration,** with people moving around the globe for jobs, education, or pleasure and adventure.

835. With this **increased mobility comes an increase in cultural exchange;** cultures are shared quickly and easily, leading to new ideas being formed, fought over, and fused,

836. **The sharing of knowledge between countries has increased** at unprecedented levels due to global connections. It is easy to access information on any subject imaginable with just a few clicks online.

837. **Globalization has helped to reduce poverty worldwide by increasing access to resources** and providing more economic opportunities for those living in developing nations.

838. **Automation is another big factor that has increased due to globalization.** Technological advancements are allowing machines or robots to do a lot of work previously done manually, leading to higher productivity at a lower cost.

839. **Carbon emissions have increased drastically since the first wave of globalization** (the Industrial Revolution). As a result, climate change has become an increasingly important issue on a global scale, with countries coming together to tackle this problem collectively.

840. **Due to its ease of use, international banking is growing rapidly.** Money can be sent from one side of the world to the other easily and securely within minutes through online platforms.

841. **Global fashion trends are constantly being shaped** by the increased flow of goods and ideas between countries.

The Fall of the Berlin Wall
(1989)

The fall of the Berlin Wall was a momentous moment in history. This chapter will uncover sixteen fascinating facts about this iconic event.

842. **The Berlin Wall was built in 1961 and divided the city of Berlin into two parts:** the communist East and the democratic West.

843. **The wall's main purpose was to stop people from crossing to West Berlin,** where the quality of life was much higher.

844. **Around three million people left East Berlin before the wall was created.**

845. In 1987, during **US President Reagan's visit to Berlin, he gave his iconic "Tear down this wall"** speech, in which he urged Mikhail Gorbachev—the leader of the USSR—to open the Berlin Wall.

846. On November 9th, 1989, citizens of both sides began **tearing down sections of the wall** with their bare hands.

847. **The fall of the Berlin Wall marked an end to Cold War tensions between East and West Germany** and eventually led to Germany's reunification in 1990.

848. **People celebrated by painting graffiti on what remained of the wall** after its destruction. Many pieces are now displayed around the world as memorials for freedom.

849. **The remains of the wall can still be seen at various places throughout Berlin today,** including **Bernauer Strasse near Checkpoint Charlie,** where tourists can take photos or even touch it!

850. **The fall symbolized not only peace but also hope for democracy in Europe and beyond.**

851. **The fall of the wall had a long-lasting effect on international relations,** significantly improving ties inside Europe. Eastern European countries were also slowly integrated into the wider democratic family of nations.

852. In December 1989, **US President George H. W. Bush declared that "the day marks a victory for freedom."**

853. **Pope John Paul II visited East Berlin in October 1989 to celebrate German reunification.** His visit was seen as instrumental in helping build bridges between East and West Germany after years of separation.

854. **Over the years, hundreds of artists have been inspired by this event** and created art to commemorate it, including sculptures, paintings, films, and literature.

855. On October 3rd, **Berlin Day is celebrated in Germany**. The day is dedicated to commemorating freedom and celebrating the reunification between East and West.

856. **The fall of the Berlin Wall showed that even in times of great political tension and conflict,** peaceful protest can lead to change.

857. **The fall of the Berlin Wall is perhaps the most iconic symbol of freedom around the world.**

The Persian Gulf War
(1990–1991)

Discover fifteen facts about one of **the most dramatic, significant, and televised military operations in world history: the Persian Gulf War.** From its inception to its conclusion, we will explore several fascinating pieces of information about this conflict between Iraq and an international coalition.

858. **The Persian Gulf War was a conflict in the Middle East** between Iraq and an international coalition of forces led by the United States.

859. It began on August 2nd, 1990, when Iraqi leader **Saddam Hussein ordered his army to invade Kuwait.**

860. A total of thirty-nine nations contributed troops or military equipment **to help liberate Kuwait from Iraq's control,** including Saudi Arabia, Egypt, Syria, and France, among others.

861. **Early fighting involved air strikes against targets in both countries.** Ground forces were largely held back until February 1991, when **Operation Desert Storm** launched a massive allied offensive into Iraq.

862. This marked the start of a one-hundred-hour-long land war, which would ultimately lead to **victory for the coalition forces over Saddam Hussein's regime** in late February 1991, a little over six months after hostilities had begun.

863. **Up to a million soldiers took part in the war effort,** making it one of the largest military operations since World War II.

864. **The US-led coalition relied heavily on the use of advanced technology,** such as precision-guided munitions, stealth aircraft, and cruise missiles.

865. **Iraqi forces used chemical weapons against Kuwaiti civilians** and coalition troops during the conflict, leading to condemnation from around the world.

866. **Nearly three million people were forced to leave their homes due to fighting in Iraq and Kuwait,** many of them refugees who had fled violence or famine in parts of Africa and Asia earlier that decade.

867. **The war ended with a ceasefire agreement that declared an end to all hostilities between Iraq and the coalition forces.** This was followed by the United Nations Security Council Resolutions (UNSCRs) placing sanctions upon Saddam Hussein's regime.

868. **The Persian Gulf War saw the first large-scale use of smart bombs in combat.** These bombs allowed for greater accuracy and fewer civilian casualties than traditional bombing missions.

869. **Estimates vary, but it is believed 400,000 Iraqi soldiers were killed or wounded,** while the coalition forces lost around 300 people in addition to about 450 Kuwaiti losses.

870. **This conflict was one of the most televised wars in history,** raising public awareness of events unfolding on faraway battlefields.

871. **Different media outlets from around the world provided millions** with unprecedented access to information on **the conflict in Iraq and Kuwait.**

872. **The conflict was a turning point in Middle Eastern history** and marked the first instance of an international coalition successfully ousting an oppressive ruler from power after **World War II,** setting a precedent for future military interventions worldwide.

The Rise of Social Media
(1990s–Present)

For centuries, humans have searched for ways to connect and share information. In the late 1990s, that search led to the inception of social media—a platform where people can communicate and express themselves in an instant. This chapter **will explore how this phenomenon has evolved** from its humble beginnings into what it is today with sixteen interesting facts.

873. **Social media is a way for people to connect and share information online.**

874. **The late 1990s and early 2000s saw the emergence of the first social media platforms.** Websites like Six Degrees and Friendster helped people make connections across the world.

875. **One of the first major social media platforms was Myspace,** launched in 2003 by **Tom Anderson and Chris DeWolfe.** The site allowed users to post music, photos, videos, and messages on personal profile pages called blogs.

876. **In 2004, Facebook was founded by Mark Zuckerberg** while he was studying at Harvard University. It eventually became one of the most popular social networks in the globe.

877. **Twitter (now called X) also started gaining traction in 2006 when Jack Dorsey** sent out its first tweet, "just setting up my twtter." This

microblogging site initially allowed users to send 140-character messages called tweets.

878. **Since then, other platforms have been created**, including **Instagram** in 2010, **Snapchat** in 2011, and **TikTok** in 2016, giving people even more ways to share their lives online.

879. **Social media platforms also provide people access to news, entertainment, and information from around the globe.** They also allow businesses to advertise their products or services.

880. **Hundreds of millions of people join social media** sites each year; the number is almost five billion today!

881. **Social media can be used for good causes.** It has been used to raise awareness about global issues such as poverty and climate change by creating campaigns that reach millions of people at once.

882. Social media has been credited with helping to spread movements like **the Arab Spring, Black Lives Matter, and the #MeToo Movement.**

883. **Some argue that excessive use of social media may lead to depression** and isolating behavior due to its addictive nature.

884. **Hashtags are words or phrases preceded by a "#" sign,** which help users categorize and search for topics on social media platforms.

885. **Social networks have become more than just a way to keep in touch with friends;** they are also used by celebrities, politicians, and influencers, allowing them to reach out directly to their fans worldwide.

886. **Another popular feature of social media is live-streaming videos,** which allow viewers from around the world to interact with content creators in real time.

887. **Many companies now use social media platforms like LinkedIn and YouTube** as part of their marketing strategy due to their wide reach across different age groups and cultures.

888. **Although we have seen a lot of positive outcomes from social media,** there is still a need for more regulation **to protect users' data and privacy.**

The Breakup of the Soviet Union
(1991)

Discover the fascinating history of the dissolution of the Soviet Union in this chapter. Learn about **sixteen interesting facts about its collapse,** including what happened to the countries that had been part of the USSR.

889. **The Soviet Union** (or USSR) **was founded after the Russian Revolution.** The Soviet Union's strength started declining during the later stages of the Cold War.

890. Before its demise in 1991, **the USSR had been the world's largest communist state.** It was comprised of fifteen republics from eastern Europe and central Asia.

891. **Mikhail Gorbachev took over as leader of the Soviet Union** in 1985 and introduced reforms like glasnost (openness) and perestroika (restructuring).

892. In 1990 and 1991, **several republics declared independence from the Soviet Union,** leading to its breakup at midnight on December 26th, 1991.

893. Georgia and Lithuania were among the first to declare independence.

894. **Following Gorbachev's resignation from office on December** 25th, 1991, Russia officially took over all remaining assets of the disbanded USSR, including nuclear weapons.

895. **Boris Yeltsin became president of Russia** after his election victory in June 1991, while other leaders emerged for their respective newly independent nations.

896. **The dissolution of the Soviet Union was one of the most complicated geopolitical events in modern history** due to its many consequences, such as political turmoil and economic collapse across eastern Europe and central Asia.

897. After the breakup of **the Soviet Union, millions of people migrated from former Soviet republics** either domestically or internationally due to a multitude of reasons, such as instability and conflict.

898. **After gaining independence, various republics established democratic systems based on market economics,** which allowed them access to global markets, promoting growth but also leading to an increase in poverty rates.

899. **The collapse of the Soviet Union led to a crisis in central Asia, eastern Europe, and Russia,** with some countries struggling due to civil wars, ethnic tensions, or corruption, like **Tajikistan**, which suffered a five-year-long civil war. It is believed **20,000 to 150,000 people were killed.**

900. **Many people of the former USSR experienced difficulties after the Soviet Union's breakup.** Wages were delayed or simply never paid out, leaving many in poverty and unable to meet basic needs, such as food, electricity, or water.

901. **The breakup of the Soviet Union caused a massive shift in the balance of power,** as communism was significantly weakened around the world.

902. **The breakup did lead world leaders toward developing ways of preventing further escalations and destabilization.**

903. The world has since seen some of **the former Soviet republics grow and become economically successful** with more freedom for their citizens, such as **Estonia**, which ranks among the top competitive economies.

904. **The breakup of the Soviet Union increased the number and diversity of languages spoken within the former USSR's borders.** Previously, people had to use Russian as their main language for communication, even outside Russia.

The War in Afghanistan
(2001–2021)

The war in Afghanistan began shortly after the terrorist attacks on the US on September 11th, 2001. In this chapter, we will explore sixteen interesting facts about this conflict, including its effects on those involved.

905. **The war in Afghanistan started in October 2001 after the terrorist attacks on September 11th, 2001.**

906. **The US, members of NATO, and other countries fought against Taliban forces and al-Qaeda terrorists** to try to keep them from attacking people in Afghanistan or anywhere else around the world.

907. **The war resulted in tens of thousands of casualties on both sides,** including many Afghan civilians.

908. **The US provided humanitarian aid worth billions of dollars to support reconstruction projects in Afghanistan** cities, helping build schools and roads and improving infrastructure for people living there.

909. **NATO provided financial assistance through trust funds,** which helped rebuild the Afghani military and police forces.

910. In 2020, there were only **about 4,500 US troops stationed there** compared to a peak of nearly 100,000 in 2011.

911. **In 2013, the US stopped leading combat operations in Afghanistan.** The Afghanis took on a leadership role.

912. **The Biden administration finally decided to withdraw from the country** in 2021. The Taliban almost immediately took control of the government after the US left.

913. **Many question if the decision to pull the military out of Afghanistan was a wise decision.**

914. **The US-led coalition suffered more than 23,000 casualties,** with about 2,400 soldiers dead and the rest wounded.

915. **The US spent over two trillion dollars on this war effort.**

916. **Although it is not known for sure how many civilians died in the war,** most sources estimate that around forty-six thousand civilians died or were injured in the war. This number does not include those who died from disease or the lack of food.

917. **By 2023, the Taliban had managed to create a very conservative Islamic state in Afghanistan.**

918. **There is a lot of poverty in parts of Afghanistan due to a lack of economic growth** because its infrastructure was heavily damaged during the conflict.

919. Today, **much of the Afghan population has been greatly affected by combat.** The living conditions are very poor, and women have almost no rights in the country.

920. **As of August 2023, no country recognizes the Taliban-led government of Afghanistan.**

The War in Iraq
(2003–2011)

This chapter will explore the Iraq War, a conflict that had far-reaching consequences. We'll take a look at **sixteen interesting facts about the war,** including its causes, outcomes, participants, and effects on Iraqi civilians.

921. **The Iraq War began on March 19th, 2003, and lasted for eight years (2011).**

922. **It was led by the US, Britain, Australia,** and some other countries as part of a coalition force to remove Saddam Hussein from power.

923. **Over 4,800 coalition troops were killed during the war,** most of them American soldiers.

924. **More than 100,000 Iraqi civilians died because of violence caused by the war,** according to estimates from **the UN High Commissioner for Refugees** (UNHCR).

925. **The war cost the US over two trillion dollars** and is considered to be one of the most expensive wars in modern history.

926. **In 2010, President Barack Obama declared an end to combat operations in Iraq** and withdrew most US troops from the country by 2011.

927. **Operation Iraqi Freedom was replaced with Operation New Dawn,** which focused on assisting government efforts against terrorism within Iraq's borders until it ended in December 2011, when most US troops were removed from Iraq.

928. **Saddam Hussein was captured on December** 13th, 2003, after a manhunt that lasted nine months since his fall from power earlier that year.

929. **Hussein was found guilty of crimes against humanity at trial and executed** on December 30th, 2006.

930. **A major goal of the war was to find weapons of mass destruction** (WMDs) that Saddam Hussein might have had, but none were ever found.

931. **The Iraq War was one of the most controversial wars in modern history** because many people argued that it should never have taken place or have ended when it did.

932. By June 2014, **the Islamic State of Iraq and Syria** (ISIS) had risen to power in the region, leading to a new war against them. As of August 2023, that war is still ongoing.

933. **The Iraq War was part of the larger "War on Terror" initiated by President George W. Bush after 9/11,** which also included military operations in Afghanistan and other Middle Eastern countries.

934. **The US has sent more than sixty billion dollars' worth of aid to help rebuild Iraq** since 2013, as well as providing humanitarian relief for millions suffering from its effects.

935. **The Iraqi people have held several democratic elections since 2004** and continue to strive toward building a peaceful future for themselves despite all they endured during this conflict period.

936. Although the **war has officially ended, its effects are still being felt in Iraq today** as people continue to live with the consequences of it and strive for a better future.

The Arab Spring
(2010–Present)

The Arab Spring was a major turning point in the history of the Middle East. This chapter will explore this important event through sixteen interesting facts about its origins, participants, and outcomes.

937. **The Arab Spring was a wave of protests, uprisings, and revolutions that spread across the Middle East** from 2010 to 2012.

938. **People wanted more freedom, basic rights, democracy, and social reforms from their governments.**

939. **It started when protesters in Tunisia ousted President Zine El Abidine Ben Ali** after twenty-three years in power in what has been dubbed the Jasmine Revolution.

940. **Protesters used peaceful demonstrations** to make their voices heard all over the region for months on end.

941. **Many countries were affected by these protests,** including Libya, Syria, Yemen, and Bahrain.

942. **Governments responded with violence against protestors,** leading to the deaths of many people.

943. **Citizens called out for help through social media sites like Facebook or Twitter,** which helped bring attention to the situation inside those repressive regimes.

944. **Women played an active role in the Arab Spring.** They protested in the streets and also participated in online campaigns to publicize their cause.

945. **Following the rebellions, certain nations conducted elections to choose new heads of state.**

946. **In some countries, the Arab Spring led to changes like increased freedom of speech,** greater rights for women, better access to education, and more open economies.

947. **In Syria, the protests eventually resulted in a destructive civil war** from which the country still suffers today.

948. In 2011, **a Nobel Peace Prize was awarded jointly to Liberian President Ellen Johnson Sirleaf, Liberian activist Leymah Gbowee, and Yemeni politician Tawakkul Karman** for their nonviolent struggle for the safety of women during the Arab Spring.

949. **The Arab Spring resulted in the overthrowing of three governments in total** and three governments making constitutional reforms.

950. **Independent international actors, like Anonymous, a hacking group, declared their support to the protesters** by helping spread the word and launching cyberattacks on government websites.

951. **The Arab Spring remains one of the most obvious demonstrations** of the power of modern technology and social media.

952. Despite its mixed results, **the Arab Spring changed the Middle East forever** and showed citizens their power to create change.

The European Migrant Crisis
(2015–Present)

This chapter will explore the European migrant crisis, a humanitarian disaster that has had far-reaching consequences on global displacement. We'll take a look at sixteen interesting facts about how this crisis began, its impact on Europe, and the efforts taken by governments to provide aid for those affected by it.

953. **The European migrant crisis** refers to the increased wave of migration beginning in 2015 when many people from **African and Middle Eastern countries** tried **to enter Europe** for safety.

954. **The majority of the people who migrated to Europe came from Syria, Afghanistan, Iraq,** and other countries in the Middle East affected by war and poverty.

955. **Tens of millions of Asian and African migrants have been entering Europe** increasingly since 2015, with Mediterranean countries, such as Greece and Italy, having the largest number of illegal immigrants.

956. **Many refugees arrived on boats or small rafts across dangerous waters to reach safer shores in Europe with their families and belongings.**

957. **Some refugees spent months walking thousands of miles** before they could find refuge in another country or return home safely if possible.

958. **Countries, including France, Germany, Italy, Spain, and Turkey, opened up their borders** to provide safe havens for these migrants seeking protection from danger at home

959. People could apply for temporary or permanent asylum, although permanent asylum depends upon an individual case.

960. Some European countries have offered special programs, like job training and language classes, to help migrants integrate into their new communities successfully.

961. The crisis has sparked debates around the world about how best to manage migration and ensure safe passage for those seeking refuge from harmful situations at home.

962. Organizations like **the United Nations High Commissioner for Refugees** (UNHCR) and Amnesty International have provided funding, resources, and workers to assist those affected by this humanitarian crisis.

963. **Different countries are currently working together** with international organizations on a global response plan that will provide more protection for refugees fleeing war-torn areas.

964. While **some governments** have agreed upon solutions, such as providing financial assistance or allowing people asylum, **many remain divided over what should be done next.**

965. **Many individuals around the world continue to show compassion toward refugees** through donations, volunteering efforts, or by participating in discussions that could help improve living conditions and better manage migration in Europe.

966. **The European Union** (EU) has been working together to address the root causes of the crisis, such as war, poverty, and inequality in other parts of the world, which are seen as significant contributors to global displacement.

967. For long-term solutions to be possible, both **governments and citizens must find more sustainable answers that can provide safety and stability** for those affected by this ongoing humanitarian disaster.

968. **The European migrant crisis has highlighted the importance of international cooperation** and compassion between countries to protect individuals who are fleeing danger or seeking a better life elsewhere.

The Syrian Civil War
(2011—Present)

This chapter will explore the devastating effects of the Syrian Civil War. We'll delve into sixteen facts about its origins, participants, and the atrocities that have been committed.

969. **The Syrian Civil War began in 2011** and is still happening as of August 2023.

970. **The war started after people in Syria protested against the government,** which was led by **President Bashar al-Assad.**

971. **Since the war began, millions of Syrians have had to leave their homes** and are now living as refugees in other countries or within Syria itself.

972. **Many different groups are fighting each other in the war,** including rebels who want change and the Syrian government forces that support Assad's rule

973. **Other countries, such as Russia, Iran, Turkey, and the US, have also been involved in the war,** sending troops to help fight on either side of the conflict.

974. **The city of Aleppo has been one of the hardest-hit areas during the civil war.** Many buildings have been destroyed by intense bombing campaigns carried out by both sides.

975. Since the conflict's beginning, **people have witnessed the use of different violent tactics,** such as suicide bombings and even the use of chemical weapons.

976. **The conflict has had a terrible impact on Syria's economy,** with people struggling to buy food or access basic services.

977. **The World Food Programme** estimates that a little over twelve million Syrians are food insecure.

978. **Many young Syrians have been left without a basic education due to the war,** as schools and universities have been destroyed or closed down.

979. **The civilian casualty toll of the Syrian Civil War is estimated to be in the hundreds of thousands.**

980. In 2014, **ISIS emerged in Syria and Iraq, adding another layer of complexity to this ongoing conflict.** ISIS is responsible for much violence against civilian populations and kidnapping people for ransom money.

981. **Most Syrian refugees live in Europe, Turkey, and Lebanon.** These places suffer from a lack of resources needed to support the refugees properly.

982. **The UN has been trying to broker a peace deal in the civil war,** but so far, there have not been any lasting agreements.

983. In 2018, **President Assad regained control of most of Syria's territory.** As of May 2023, it is believed he holds around 65 percent of the country.

984. **Despite the end of major combat operations, violence still occurs on both sides,** including airstrikes that kill civilians and clashes with rebel groups who want change in Syria.

The Climate Crisis
(2020—Present)

The climate crisis is an issue that affects everyone, from rising sea levels to extreme weather events. In this chapter, we will take a look at sixteen facts about the climate crisis and how it has impacted our planet since 2020.

985. **The climate crisis is a long-term change in the planet's weather patterns** caused by human activities, such as burning fossil fuels and cutting down forests.

986. **Climate change has been happening for years,** but it's getting worse and more urgent because of our pollution levels and emissions of heat-trapping gases like carbon dioxide (CO2).

987. **Because of climate change, some areas are getting warmer while others are getting colder,** making extreme temperatures more common all over the world.

988. **Heat waves, heavy rainfall, and drought can cause food shortages in some places,** which puts people at risk of hunger and poverty if they don't have enough to eat or money to buy food.

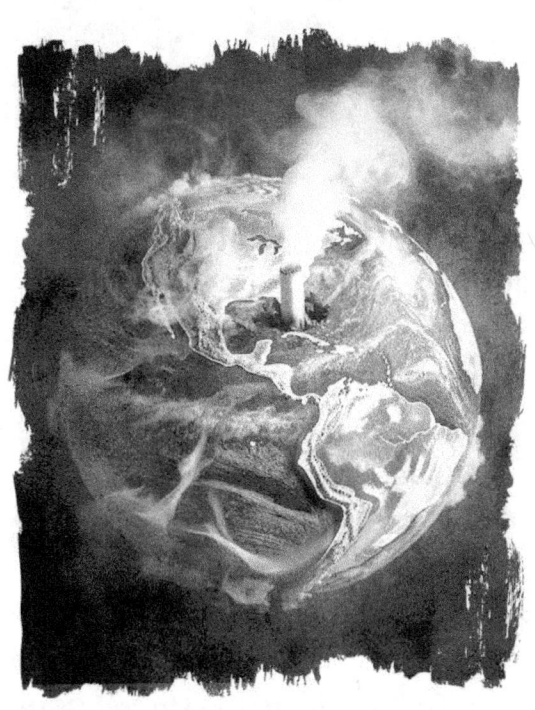

989. **Sea levels around the world have risen significantly due to melting ice caps** at both poles; this means that many coastal communities are threatened by flooding from storms or high tides during strong hurricanes and typhoons.

990. **Climate change has caused more frequent and intense hurricanes, floods, droughts, heatwaves, and wildfires,** which can have devastating impacts on people's lives.

991. **Climate change is causing changes in ecosystems,** such as coral reefs dying off due to ocean acidification or animals adapting to new climates to survive.

992. Climate change is making the air we breathe more polluted, as there are higher levels of smog and ozone, which harm people's health.

993. The climate crisis affects everyone around the world, from small island nations threatened by **rising sea levels** to cities suffering from extreme drought conditions leading to water shortages.

994. Reducing energy consumption through better insulation, lighting fixtures, and appliances and using renewable energies like hydroelectricity can help ease the effects of climate change.

995. By cutting down on pollution-causing activities (like burning fossil fuels), **the world can reduce greenhouse gas emissions,** which are the main causes of climate change.

996. Making sustainable choices, such as eating a plant-based diet, avoiding single-use plastics, buying local produce, and investing in green energy solutions, **can help reduce our carbon footprint.**

997. The Paris Climate Accords, which was signed by 196 parties, is the most comprehensive international treaty on climate change.

998. Today, **China, the United States, and India are among the world's biggest polluters** due to their large population sizes and inability to produce green energy on a large enough scale.

999. Sweden and Denmark are the greenest countries and promote sustainability on a large scale.

1000. **Though the Paris Agreement** (also known as the Paris Climate Accords) was an important step in the right direction when it came **to raising international awareness regarding climate change,** many experts claim that more commitment and action are needed by the signatories to reach the goals set by **the Climate Accords.**

Conclusion

We have now seen the incredible impact that human beings have had on the world throughout history. Our ancestors created civilizations and religions, **invented tools and technologies, explored new lands and ideas,** and fought wars for freedom or power; all of these experiences have shaped us as a species, and many of these things are still happening today.

This book has explored how humans interact with their environment to create inventions such as fire, the domestication of animals, and writing. Various periods have brought amazing things to life, such as art during **the Renaissance** and the **pyramids of ancient Egypt.** The world has witnessed massive devastation in the world wars, but it has also seen that peace can be achieved.

The world still has much to overcome, as can be demonstrated by the recent Arab Spring and the European migrant crisis. We are living through history right now, so it is important to continue learning about the past to better understand why we are where we are today.

If you enjoyed this book, a review on Amazon would be greatly appreciated because it would mean a lot to hear from you.

To leave a review:

1. Open your camera app.
2. Point your mobile device at the QR code.
3. The review page will appear in your web browser.

Thanks for your support!

Check out another book in the series

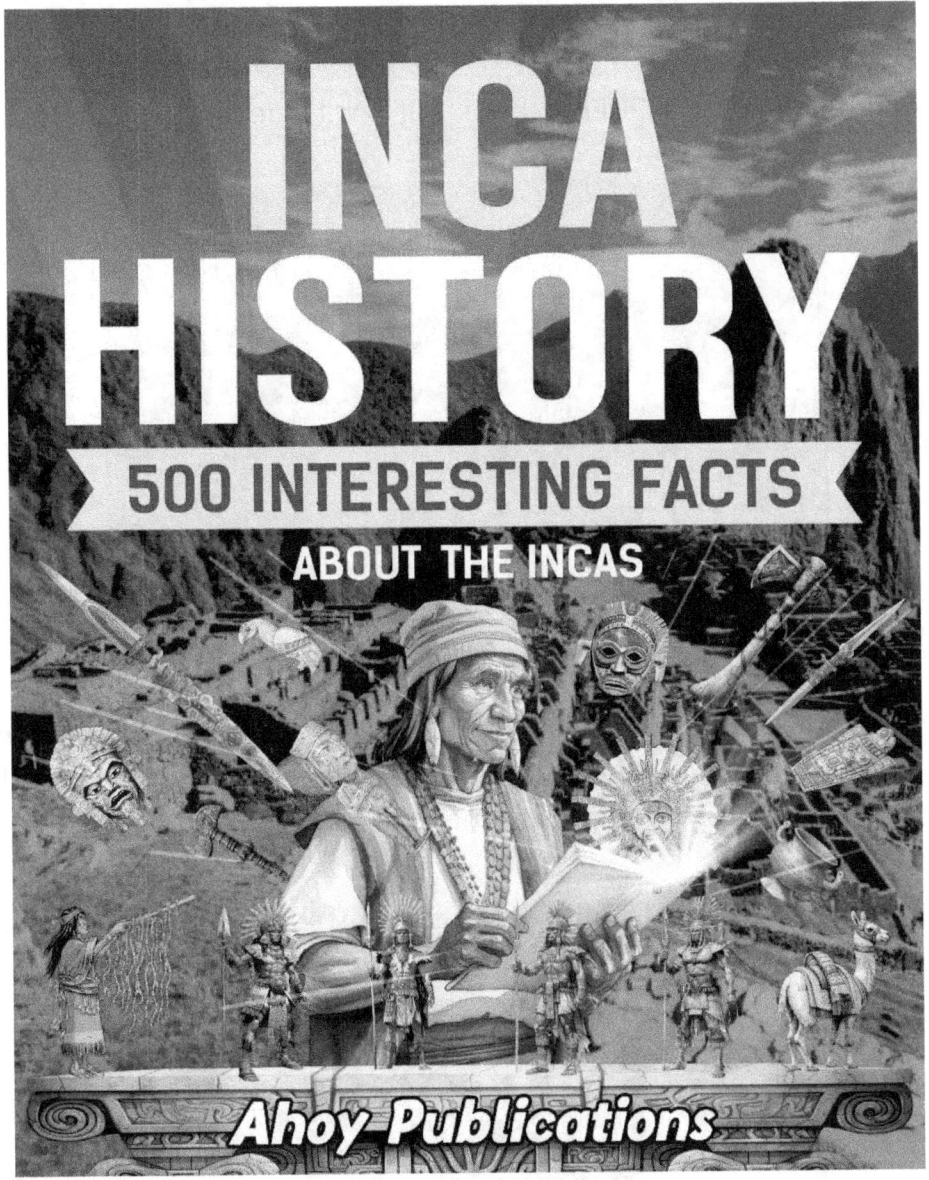

Welcome Aboard, Check Out This Limited-Time Free Bonus!

Ahoy, reader! Welcome to the Ahoy Publications family, and thanks for snagging a copy of this book! Since you've chosen to join us on this journey, we'd like to offer you something special.

Check out the link below for a FREE e-book filled with delightful facts about American History.

But that's not all - you'll also have access to our exclusive email list with even more free e-books and insider knowledge. Well, what are ye waiting for? Click the link below to join and set sail toward exciting adventures in American History.

Access your bonus here: <u>https://ahoypublications.com/</u>

Or, Scan the QR code!

Sources and Additional References

1. "Human Evolution Facts & Summary - Hominid Species." Encyclopedia Britannica Online Academic Edition, Nov 2018, www.encyclopediabritannica.com/topic/human-evolution#ref83598

2. "How DNA Analysis is Rewriting History of First People in Australia - BBC News." BBC, Feb 2017 https://www.bbc.com/news/world-australia-38904574.

3. "How DNA Analysis is Rewriting History of First People in Australia - BBC News." BBC, Feb 2017 https://www.bbc.com/news/world-australia-38904574

4. "Domestication Of Animals." History, history.com Staff, 2021, www.history.com/topics/prehistory/domestication-of-animals/.

5. "Ancient Civilizations: Timeline & Characteristics." Ancient History Encyclopedia, ancient.eu/civilization/.

6. "Roman Empire: Overview of the Roman Republic and Empire." Khan Academy, www.khanacademyorg/humanities/world-history/ancient-medieval1/roman-empire1/a/overview-of -the-roman-republic-and-empire.

7. "Ancient Greece: Overview of Classical Greek Period." Khan Academy., https://wwwkhanacademyorg/humanities/world-history/ancient-medieval1/greek classical-period/-a//overview-of-classical-greek-period.

8. "Vedic Civilization." Encyclopedia Britannica. https://www.britannica.com/topic/ Vedic-civilization.

9. "Assyrian Empire: Overview & History" Khan Academy, https://wwwkhanacademyorg/humanities/world-history/ancientmedieval1/assyria-neo – assyrian – empire/a//overview-of-assyria-neo-assryian-empire.

10. "Nubian Civilization." Encyclopedia Britannica., https://www.britannicacom /topic/Nubian – civilization.

11. "Ancient China." Ancient History Encyclopedia, https://www.ancienteu//china/.

12. "Maya Civilization." Encyclopedia Britannica, https://www.britannica.com/topic/ Maya-civilization.

13. "Inca Empire." Encyclopedia Britannica. https:// www.britannica.com/topic/Inca-empire.

14. "Aztecs." Encyclopedia Britannica. https://www.britannica.com/topic/Aztecs.

15. "Mesopotamia." Encyclopedia Britannica, https://www.britannica.com/place /Mesopotamia-ancient-region-Asia/Inventions#ref255748.

16. Lehner, Mark and Gary Stickel eds., The Complete Pyramids: Solving the Ancient Mysteries (London: Thames & Hudson).

17. Drielen, Jelle Van and Marlies Heinen eds., 2000 BC: The Bruce Trigger Book of Ancient Civilizations (Montreal: McGill-Queen's University Press)

18. "Ancient Egypt: An Overview." Ancient History Encyclopedia, ancient.eu/Egypt/, 2020.

19. "The Bronze Age." History.com, A&E Television Networks, 2020, http://www.history.com/topics/pre-history/bronze-age.

20. "Ancient Greece." Encyclopedia Britannica, Encyclopedia Britannica, Inc., https://www.britannica.com/place/ancient-Greece.

21. "Barbarian Invasions." Encyclopedia Britannica Online Academic Edition/Encyclopedia Britannica Inc., 2019. www.britannica.com/event/barbarian-invasions#ref76591.

22. Gibbon, Edward. The Decline and the Fall of the Roman Empire. Penguin Classics, 2000.

23. Mackay Christopher S. The Mongols in World History. (Oxford University Press, 2011).

24. "Renaissance." Encyclopedia Britannica, https://www.britannica.com/event/ Renaissance-European-history.

25. "The Scientific Revolution." History.com, A&E Television Networks, 2010, www.history.com/topics/the-scientific-revolution.

26. "Age of Enlightenment (1650-1800)." Encyclopedia Britannica Online Academic Edition., https://www.britannica/com/event/Age-of-Enlightenment-1650-1800#ref140967.

27. Miller, John C., The Revolutionary War: A Concise History from 1763 to 1783. (New York: Oxford University Press, 2012).

28. Craig, Robert L. "The Industrial Revolution." Encyclopedia Britannica, Encyclopedia Britannica, Inc., 2015, www.britannica.com/event/Industrial-Revolution#ref2029816.

29. "Civil War Statistics and Facts." National Parks Service, U.S. Department of the Interior, https://www.nps.gov/civilwar/facts-and-figures-stats-on-the-american-.htm.

30. Anderson, Jenny. "World War I (WW1): Causes and Timeline." History Hit, 20 Mar. 2020, www.historyhit.com/world-war-one/.

31. Gjelten, Tom. "The Role of The February Revolution in Russia's History." NPR, NPR, 2017, www.npr.org/2017/03/08/519160968/the-role-of-the-february-revolution-in-russiashistory.

32. Encyclopedia Britannica. "Great Depression." Encyclopedia Britannica, The Editors of Encyclopedia Britannica, 2021, www.britannica.com/event/Great-Depression.

33. "World War II Facts: Timeline, Causes & Major Events." History Hit, www.historyhit.com/world-war-two/.

34. Brinkley, Alan, et al., eds. The Unfinished Nation: A Concise History of the American People (New York: McGraw Hill Higher Education), 2017.

35. "Cuban Revolution." Encyclopedia Britannica, https://www.britannica.com/ event/Cuban-Revolution#ref188919.

36. "Mikhail Gorbachev." Britannica, The Editors of Encyclopedia Britannica, https://www.britannica.com/biography/Mikhail-Gorbachev.